*My **H**eart Is At Ease*

THE AZRIELI SERIES OF HOLOCAUST SURVIVOR MEMOIRS:
PREVIOUSLY PUBLISHED TITLES

ENGLISH TITLES

Album of My Life by Ann Szedlecki
Bits and Pieces by Henia Reinhartz
A Drastic Turn of Destiny by Fred Mann
E/96: Fate Undecided by Paul-Henri Rips
Fleeing from the Hunter by Marian Domanski
From Generation to Generation by Agnes Tomasov
Gatehouse to Hell by Felix Opatowski
Getting Out Alive by Tommy Dick
If, By Miracle by Michael Kutz
If Home Is Not Here by Max Bornstein
If Only It Were Fiction by Elsa Thon
In Hiding by Marguerite Élias Quddus
Knocking on Every Door by Anka Voticky
Little Girl Lost by Betty Rich
Memories from the Abyss by William Tannenzapf / *But I Had a Happy
    Childhood* by Renate Krakauer
The Shadows Behind Me by Willie Sterner
Spring's End by John Freund
Suddenly the Shadow Fell by Leslie Meisels with Eva Meisels
Survival Kit by Zuzana Sermer
Tenuous Threads by Judy Abrams / *One of the Lucky Ones*
    by Eva Felsenburg Marx
Under the Yellow and Red Stars by Alex Levin
Vanished Boyhood by George Stern
The Violin by Rachel Shtibel / *A Child's Testimony* by Adam Shtibel
W Hour by Arthur Ney
We Sang in Hushed Voices by Helena Jockel

TITRES FRANÇAIS

L'Album de ma vie par Ann Szedlecki
L'Antichambre de l'enfer par Felix Opatowski
Cachée par Marguerite Elias Quddus
Citoyen de nulle part par Max Bornstein
Étoile jaune, étoile rouge par Alex Levin
La Fin du printemps par John Freund
Fragments de ma vie par Henia Reinhartz
Frapper à toutes les portes par Anka Voticky
De génération en génération par Agnes Tomasov
Matricule E/96 par Paul-Henri Rips
Objectif : survivre par Tommy Dick
Retenue par un fil par Judy Abrams/ *Une question de chance* par Eva
  Felsenburg Marx
Seule au monde par Betty Rich
Souvenirs de l'abîme par William Tannenzapf/ *Le Bonheur de l'innocence*
  par Renate Krakauer
Un terrible revers de fortune par Fred Mann
Traqué par Marian Domanski
Le Violon par Rachel Shtibel/ *Témoignage d'un enfant*
  par Adam Shtibel

My Heart Is At Ease
Gerta Solan

THE AZRIELI FOUNDATION
www.azrielifoundation.org

Cover and book design by Mark Goldstein
Endpaper maps by Martin Gilbert
Map on page xxxi by François Blanc

LIBRARY AND ARCHIVES CANADA CATALOGUING IN PUBLICATION

Solan, Gerta, 1929–, author
       My heart is at ease / Gerta Solan.

(The Azrieli series of Holocaust survivor memoirs; 6)
Includes bibliographical references and index.
ISBN 978-1-897470-46-6 (pbk.)

1. Solan, Gerta, 1929–. 2. Holocaust, Jewish (1939–1945) – Czechoslovakia –
Personal narratives. 3. Jews – Czechoslovakia – Biography. 4. Holocaust survivors
– Canada – Biography. 5. Czechoslovakia – Biography. I. Azrieli Foundation,
issuing body II. Title. III. Series: Azrieli series of Holocaust survivor memoirs.
Series VI

DS135 C97 S67 2014   940.53'18092   C2014-903971-9

PRINTED IN CANADA

The Azrieli Series of Holocaust Survivor Memoirs

Naomi Azrieli, Publisher

Jody Spiegel, Program Director
Arielle Berger, Managing Editor
Elizabeth Lasserre, Senior Editor, French-Language Editions
Aurélien Bonin, French-Language Education, Outreach and Events
Catherine Person, Quebec Educational Outreach and Events
Elin Beaumont, English-language Educational Outreach and Events
Tim MacKay, New Media and Marketing

Susan Roitman, Executive Coordinator (Toronto)
Mary Mellas, Executive Coordinator (Montreal)
Eric Bélisle, Administrative Assistant

Mark Goldstein, Art Director
François Blanc, Cartographer
Bruno Paradis, Layout, French-language editions

Contents

Series Preface   xi
About the Glossary   xiii
Introduction *by Tatjana Lichtenstein*   xv

Map   xxxi

Author's Preface   1
A Carefree Childhood   3
Facing the Unknown   13
Surviving the Unbearable   25
Going Home   37
The Post-war Years   43
Another Difficult Political Era   53
Uninvited Visitors   63
Culture Shock   69
Establishing Ourselves   83
Milestones   95
Coping with Loss   107
On My Own   121
Epilogue   137

Glossary   141
Photographs   151
Index   165

Series Preface:
In their own words...

In telling these stories, the writers have liberated themselves. For so many years we did not speak about it, even when we became free people living in a free society. Now, when at last we are writing about what happened to us in this dark period of history, knowing that our stories will be read and live on, it is possible for us to feel truly free. These unique historical documents put a face on what was lost, and allow readers to grasp the enormity of what happened to six million Jews – one story at a time.

David J. Azrieli, C.M., C.Q., M.Arch
Holocaust survivor and founder, The Azrieli Foundation

Since the end of World War II, over 30,000 Jewish Holocaust survivors have immigrated to Canada. Who they are, where they came from, what they experienced and how they built new lives for themselves and their families are important parts of our Canadian heritage. The Azrieli Foundation's Holocaust Survivor Memoirs Program was established to preserve and share the memoirs written by those who survived the twentieth-century Nazi genocide of the Jews of Europe and later made their way to Canada. The program is guided by the conviction that each survivor of the Holocaust has a remarkable story to tell, and that such stories play an important role in education about tolerance and diversity.

Millions of individual stories are lost to us forever. By preserving the stories written by survivors and making them widely available to a broad audience, the Azrieli Foundation's Holocaust Survivor Memoirs Program seeks to sustain the memory of all those who perished at the hands of hatred, abetted by indifference and apathy. The personal accounts of those who survived against all odds are as different as the people who wrote them, but all demonstrate the courage, strength, wit and luck that it took to prevail and survive in such terrible adversity. The memoirs are also moving tributes to people – strangers and friends – who risked their lives to help others, and who, through acts of kindness and decency in the darkest of moments, frequently helped the persecuted maintain faith in humanity and courage to endure. These accounts offer inspiration to all, as does the survivors' desire to share their experiences so that new generations can learn from them.

The Holocaust Survivor Memoirs Program collects, archives and publishes these distinctive records and the print editions are available free of charge to libraries, educational institutions and Holocaust-education programs across Canada. They are also available for sale to the general public at bookstores. All revenues to the Azrieli Foundation from the sales of the Azrieli Series of Holocaust Survivor Memoirs go toward the publishing and educational work of the memoirs program.

The Azrieli Foundation would like to express appreciation to the following people for their invaluable efforts in producing this book: Sherry Dodson (Maracle Press), Sir Martin Gilbert, Farla Klaiman, Andrea Knight, Therese Parent, and Margie Wolfe and Emma Rodgers of Second Story Press.

About the Glossary

The following memoir contains a number of terms, concepts and historical references that may be unfamiliar to the reader. For information on major organizations; significant historical events and people; geographical locations; religious and cultural terms; and foreign-language words and expressions that will help give context and background to the events described in the text, please see the glossary beginning on page 141.

Introduction

Gerta Solan (née Gelbkopf) was born in Prague in 1929. She grew up an only child in a large, extended Jewish family whose branches connected kin in Prague, Brno and Vienna, an extended family that crisscrossed national borders and cultural boundaries. Her parents, Grete and Theodor Gelbkopf, were as much at home in Vienna as they were in Prague.

During Gerta's childhood, Prague was the capital of Czechoslovakia, a state created in 1918 and made up of territories from both the Austrian and Hungarian part of the former Habsburg Empire.[1] The First Czechoslovak Republic (1918–1938) was a multinational state dominated by Czechs and Slovaks, but inhabited by significant minority populations of Germans, Hungarians, Jews, Ruthenians and Poles. In total, Jews made up less than 3 per cent of Czechoslovakia's population. The majority of the country's Jews lived in the eastern regions, Slovakia (136,737) and Subcarpathian Ruthenia (102,542). In the west, the Bohemian Lands (Bohemia, Moravia and Silesia) were home to more than 117,000 Jews. The largest Jewish community in this part of the country was in Prague.

---

1 Tatjana Lichtenstein, "Czechoslovakia," in *The Cambridge Dictionary of Jewish History and Culture*, edited by Judith Baskin (New York: Cambridge University Press, 2011), 121–123, here 121.

XVI MY HEART IS AT EASE

As a result of the post-World War I amalgamation of these cultur-ally diverse territories, the Jews of Czechoslovakia belonged to many linguistic, national and social communities. Religious differences be-tween Jews, ranging from non-observant to Orthodox and Hasidic, were very significant. In the Bohemian Lands, Czech and German were the dominant languages among Jews while in Slovakia and fur-ther east, Jews spoke Hungarian, German, Slovak and Yiddish.[2]

In many ways, Gerta Solan's parents and their families embod-ied typical characteristics of Jewish society in the Bohemian Lands. They were urban, acculturated, German- and Czech- speaking and middle class, and had strong social and professional links to Vienna, the former Habsburg capital, now the capital of Austria. Gerta's par-ents had deep ties to Vienna. Her mother's family, the Roubitscheks, was from Bohemia, but her mother, Grete, and her five siblings were born and grew up in Vienna. Gerta's father, Theodor Gelbkopf, was from Brünn/Brno, the largest city in Moravia, and went to Vienna in pursuit of education. After they married in 1928, Grete and The-odor settled in Prague. Thus, even though the border had changed, the social and cultural ties that existed between villages and cities in the Bohemian Lands and the former imperial capital in Vienna per-sisted, held together not only by a shared German-language culture but also by extended family connections. While Prague and Vienna were capitals of Czechoslovakia and Austria respectively, economic, cultural and familial bonds remained strong.

The 1920s and '30s in Czechoslovakia are often remembered as a "golden age," a respite between two devastating wars. In an unstable and crisis-ridden Central Europe, Czechoslovakia was a relatively

---

2   For Jews in Slovakia, see Rebekah Klein-Pejšová, *Mapping Jewish Loyalties in Interwar Slovakia* (Bloomington: Indiana University Press, 2015); and for Subcar-pathian Ruthenia, see Yeshayahu A. Jelinek, *The Carpathian Diaspora: The Jews of Subcarpathian Rus and Mukachevo, 1848–1948* (New York: East European Mono-graphs, 2007).

stable and prosperous democracy. For Jews, it was important that the country's elite rejected the calls for state-sponsored antisemitism that occurred elsewhere. Indeed, conditions for Jews were radically different from those in neighbouring Hungary, Poland and, of course, Germany. Antisemitism, however, was not absent in Czechoslovakia.[3] For example, some Czech and Slovak politicians and journalists accused Jews of being disloyal citizens and agents of the old dominant elites, the country's German and Hungarian minorities. Some Czechs criticized Jews for using the German language, accusing them of deep-seated hostility toward Czechs and playing up antisemitic stereotypes to cast Jews as dangerous and perpetual outsiders. Similarly, in Slovakia, social, economic and religious tensions between Jews and Catholics persisted and by the 1930s were fuelled by some Slovak nationalists' deepening ideological and political ties to Nazi Germany.[4]

By the mid-1930s, political tensions increased between the Czech-dominated central government in Prague, Slovak nationalists and the country's large German minority. In Prague, as seven-year-old Gerta started school, her teachers instructed her and her classmates not to speak German in public so as not to become targets of people's anti-German opinions. Although there were efforts to resolve the internal strife, Adolf Hitler, the leader of Germany, pre-empted such efforts by securing an internationally-sanctioned annexation of Czechoslovakia's western border regions, the Sudetenland, in October 1938.

During the months of political crisis and uncertainty that followed, thousands of refugees, many of whom were Jews, began pouring into the Bohemian Lands from the border areas. The Jewish refugees were not welcomed by the new, more radical Czech nationalist

---

3 Michal Frankl, 'Emancipace od Židů': Český antisemitismus na konci 19. století (Praha: Paseka, 2008).

4 For a study of Slovak Catholic nationalism, see James Mace Ward, Priest, Politician, Collaborator: Jozef Tiso and the Making of Fascist Slovakia (Ithaca: Cornell University Press, 2013).

government in Prague or by many ordinary Czechs. Now, along with thousands of Jewish refugees from Austria and Germany, who had initially found a safe haven in Czechoslovakia, large numbers of Bohemian and Moravian Jews sought to escape the threat of Nazism.[5]

The following spring, on March 15, 1939, Czechoslovakia disappeared from the map when the Nazis occupied the territory and divided it among three different states. Most of the Bohemian Lands were incorporated into Nazi Germany as the Protectorate of Bohemia and Moravia. At the same time, with German support, an independent, authoritarian Catholic Slovak state appeared in parts of Slovakia. Hungary annexed parts of southern Slovakia and all of Subcarpathian Ruthenia. By 1939, the Jews of the Bohemian Lands were under direct German control while the Jews of the former eastern provinces were in the hands of hostile and openly antisemitic German allies.

In the Bohemian Lands, anti-Jewish legislation modelled on that which had been previously implemented in Germany took effect immediately. Directive after directive robbed Jews of their livelihoods, enforced social isolation and put in place a myriad of degrading rules that over time created "a ghetto without walls."[6] Jews were subject to curfews and were barred from parks, playgrounds and certain streets. Gerta Solan, along with thousands of other Jewish children, now flocked to Jewish cemeteries in search of welcoming playgrounds and friends. By August 1940, Jewish children had to attend Jewish-

---

5 For a thorough study of refugees in Czechoslovakia in the 1930s, see Kateřina Čapková and Michal Frankl, *Nejisté* útočiště: *Československo a uprchlíci před nacismem 1933–1938* (Praha: Paseka, 2008). For a shorter, English-language version, see Kateřina Čapková, "Czechoslovakia as sanctuary for refugees from Nazism," 149–159, in *Exile in Prague and Czechoslovakia, 1918–1938*, edited by Ilona Bariková et al. (Prague: Pražská edice 2005).

6 Benjamin Frommer, *The Ghetto Without Walls: The Identification, Isolation, and Elimination of Bohemian and Moravian Jewry, 1938–1945* (forthcoming).

only schools, which struggled to accommodate larger numbers of students. In Prague, the Jewish sports clubs Hagibor and Maccabi became centres for Jewish life as teachers and youth leaders tried to create a sense of normalcy and dignity for the city's Jewish children. By September 1941, Jews had to wear the yellow star in public, a sign that made their Jewishness visible in ways that felt frightening to some, humiliating to others.[7]

Unlike in German-occupied Poland, where Jews were forced into ghettos from October 1939, Jews in the Protectorate of Bohemia and Moravia, as in Germany itself, were not confined to sealed residential districts until late 1941. Living among non-Jews, they experienced what the historian Marion Kaplan has called "social death," isolated from society at large and forced into a permanent state of humiliation.[8] Yet even as German authorities and local sympathizers sought to degrade Jews, individuals like Gerta's mother managed to defy them in different ways. At times, Grete Gelbkopf refused to abide by the strict curfew imposed on Jews. Relying on the prevalence of stereotypes about Jews' physical appearance, she, a confident, elegant woman, managed to pass as a non-Jew. However, acts of everyday defiance mounted by individuals and by Jewish groups were no match for the German authorities. Beginning in October 1941, thousands of Jews from the Protectorate's largest cities were sent to ghettos and labour camps in Poland and the Baltic states. By December 1941, the Germans began deporting Jews to the fortress town Theresienstadt/ Terezín, sixty-five kilometres northwest of Prague, which was from then on to serve as a ghetto for the Protectorate's Jewish population.

Until the German occupation, Terezín had served as a military garrison with a population of about 7,000 civilians and military

7 Helena Petrův, *Zákonné bezpráví: Židé v Protektorátu Čechy a Morava* (Praha: Auditorium, 2011).

8 Marion A. Kaplan, *Between Dignity and Despair: Jewish Life in Nazi Germany* (New York: Oxford University Press, 1999).

personnel. Built to house troops, the town largely consisted of bar-racks that the Germans re-named after various German cities and regions such as Hamburg, Magdeburg, Hannover and Dresden. The three-storey buildings, covering an entire block, housed thousands of people. Over the course of 1942, more than 60,000 men, women and children of all ages from towns and cities across Bohemia and Moravia were forced into the ghetto. They were joined by thousands of Jewish deportees from Germany, Austria, the Netherlands and Denmark.[9] The ghetto population suffered tremendously from the overcrowded, inadequate living quarters, horrendous hygienic con-ditions, and starvation. These catastrophic living conditions would eventually result in the death of more than 33,000 people, about a quarter of the 140,000 Jews who were deported to Terezín between December 1941 and April 1945.[10]

Gerta and her parents were deported to Terezín on June 20, 1942.[11] Both her maternal and paternal grandparents were also deported to the ghetto.[12] It was particularly difficult for the elderly in the ghetto.

---

9 For overviews of the deportations to and from Terezín, see Karel Lagus and Josef Polák, *Město za mřížemi* (Praha: Baset, 2006 (first published 1964)).

10 For an excellent online resource on Terezín that has articles, documents and information about victims, see www.holocaust.cz/en/victims

11 Gerta's parents, Bohdan (Theodor) and Greta Gelbkopf, were, according to the official records, deported from Prague to Terezín on June 20, 1942. For this and more information, see www.holocaust.cz/en/main

12 Zikmund and Amálie Gelbkopf, Gerta's paternal grandparents, were deported from Brünn/Brno to Terezín on March 29, 1942. Zikmund Gelbkopf died in the ghetto only a few months later at the age of eighty-two. Amálie Gelbkopf passed away the following summer, in July 1943, also in Terezín. She was seventy-six years old. For specific information about the Gelbkopfs, see the victims' database on www.holocaust.cz/en/main

13 The effect of the fear of the transports is vividly described in the fascinating memoir by Norbert Troller, *Theresienstadt: Hitler's Gift to the Jews* (Chapel Hill: University of North Carolina Press, 1991)

Many had arrived from Germany and Austria without younger family members to provide support. But even for families like Gerta's, the younger generations found it difficult to help their aging relatives. Gerta could do little more than witness the suffering of her starving grandfather, much like her mother was helpless in the face of a guard's violence against her own father.

In Terezín, as in other ghettos, the German authorities designated a Jewish administration, a Council of Elders, to implement German orders and oversee housing, labour and food distribution. Most painfully, the Council was formally charged with organizing thousands of people to be deported to "the East." These transports began in January 1942, only weeks after the ghetto had been established. The transports were a source of perpetual fear as people desperately used any connection they had to someone in the ghetto administration, a group that was "protected" from deportations, to prevent themselves and their loved ones from being sent away.[13]

The Jewish Council could merely mitigate, not alleviate, the circumstances for Jews in the ghetto. As part of their efforts to better the situation for the thousands of children in Terezín, the leadership designated certain buildings as children's homes. Here, teachers, artists, athletic coaches and teenage youth leaders worked to create an environment where children could learn and play, an effort to shield the ghetto's youngest from the devastation surrounding them.[14] In seeking to create a healthy atmosphere, the ghetto leaders assigned youngsters like Gerta work in the vegetable gardens, which allowed them not only fresh air, but also access to extra food. As Gerta describes, at times, she and the other children were determined to block out the horrible conditions in the ghetto and will some sense of nor-

14 For a collection of drawings and poetry by children in Terezín, see Hana Volav-ková, ed., *I Never Saw Another Butterfly: Children's Drawings and Poems from the Terezín Concentration Camp, 1942–1944* (New York: Schocken Books, 1994).

malcy. She writes, "We were hungry for a normal life we did not have, but in our little dreams, we tried to forget reality."

Most ghettos in German-occupied territory were destroyed and their populations murdered over the course of 1942 and early 1943. Only a few that were considered particularly valuable to the German war effort, such as the ghetto in Lodz/Litzmannstadt, were preserved. Terezín's continued existence was not attributed to any particularly important manufacturing industry, but rather to its utility in the Germans' ongoing campaign to deceive their victims and outside observers about the fate of the tens of thousands of Jews "resettled in the East." Always attentive to public opinion at home, the German authorities depicted Terezín as a "retirement settlement" for elderly German and Austrian Jews.[15] The deception was extreme: Terezín was never intended to be the final destination for these elderly Jews nor for the thousands of Jews from the Bohemian Lands who were sent there.

At one point, the ghetto also served as a destination for Jews of international prominence or highly decorated Jewish war veterans, whose disappearance might bring unwelcome attention. In the summer of 1943, when the majority of the victims of the Holocaust were already dead and when evidence of mass murder was rampant, the German authorities allowed the German and the International Red Cross to visit Terezín. These visits were meant to assure anyone concerned about the fate of the deported Jews that they had indeed been resettled in "self-governing Jewish towns."

In preparation for the Red Cross visits, particularly the one in June 1944, the ghetto went through a beautification campaign. It in-

15 There are several articles covering different aspects of the ghetto in the Holocaust Encyclopedia available online through the United States Holocaust Memorial Museum; see www.ushmm.org/learn/

volved creating the appearance of a normal city with cafes, bakeries and cultural events, as well as the deportation of thousands of people to the killing centre at Auschwitz-Birkenau. This was done both to alleviate the overcrowding in the ghetto and to remove people whose bodies were visibly marked by the effects of living in Terezín. In the wake of the June 1944 visit, the German authorities forced one of the inmates, the well-known German Jewish actor and director Kurt Gerron (1897–1944), to create a propaganda film with the working title "Theresienstadt: A Documentary Film from the Jewish Settlement Area." One of the aspects of the ghetto that featured prominently in the film was its cultural life, especially musical and theatre performances.[16]

From the outset, German authorities had tolerated some educational and cultural activities in the ghetto. At first, it was seen as a way of pacifying the inmates during the first months of upheaval. Over time, concerts, lectures and theatre performances became incorporated into the propaganda image of Terezín as a normal town. By March 1943, the "Leisure Time Department" was tasked with organizing cultural life in the ghetto including orchestras. As Gerta remembers, her father was able to play the violin in one of the orchestras.

Today, the ghetto in Terezín is perhaps most well-known for its cultural life, something survivors and historians remember as acts of resistance against the denigration imposed by the Germans. Ghetto inmates, suffering from starvation, disease and terrible loss, wrote, produced and performed plays, concerts and operas, including the children's opera *Brundibár*. Artists produced "legal" drawings and paintings while secretly documenting the terrible suffering in the ghetto. At the time, however, this cultural life was fraught with ten-

---

16 An excellent documentary about Kurt Gerron and the making of the propaganda film is *Prisoner of Paradise* (PBS/Menemsha Films, 2002).

sion and some observed it with a degree of discomfort. Egon Redlich (1916–1944), who was head of the Youth Department and thus part of the ghetto elite, wrote in his diary in the summer of 1942: "So many contrasts in life here. In the yard, a cabaret with singers and in the house the old and sick are dying. Great contrasts. The young are full of desire to have a full life and the old are left without a place and without rest."[17] On the one hand, Redlich worried about art as a form of escape that would allow stronger inmates to ignore the plight of the ghetto's weakest. On the other, he understood that a cultural life, whether as escape, entertainment or spiritual experience, was important for people to fend off complete despair. This was especially important as the dreaded transports "to the East," as well as hunger and disease, continued to tear families and communities of friends apart.

From the very beginning of the Terezín ghetto's existence, trains had left with 1,000 people or more to destinations unknown to the deportees. Sometimes transports left several times a month; other times, there would be several months between transports. Beginning in January 1942, people were deported to other ghettos and camps in Poland and German-occupied Soviet territory. Between early January and late October 1942, more than 42,000 people were deported to ghettos, labour camps and killing centres in places such as Riga, Warsaw, Minsk, Maly Trostinec (near Minsk) and Treblinka.[18] From late October 1942 onwards, all transports were directed to Auschwitz. In all, almost 45,000 people were sent from Terezín to Auschwitz.[19]

In September 1943, after almost a seven-month break in deportations, about 5,000 men, women and children were deported to Aus-

---

17 *The Terezín Diary of Gonda Redlich*, edited by Saul S. Friedman (Lexington: University of Kentucky Press, 1992), 58 (entry for July 19, 1942).

18 Lagus and Polák, *Město za mřížemi*, 251-252

19 Lagus and Polák, *Město za mřížemi*, 252 and Vojtěch Blodig, *Terezín in "the Final Solution of the Jewish Question"* (Prague: Oswald, 2006), 33.

chwitz. Unlike other transports that arrived in the work camp and killing centre Auschwitz II (Birkenau), the deportees did not undergo a selection, nor were men and women separated. Instead, the prisoners were allocated a separate area in Birkenau, which became known as the Czech or Terezín "family camp."[20] For months, the Terezín inmates were kept together. Then, on March 8 and 9, 1944, the Terezín family camp was "liquidated," its inhabitants murdered. From then on, when transports arrived from Terezín, the people aboard underwent a selection on the arrival platform and the majority were sent straight to their deaths in the nearby gas chambers.

On October 23, 1944, Gerta Solan and her mother were on the second-to-last transport that left Terezín. Gerta's mother, having worked in the housing department for the ghetto administration, had been in one of the groups "protected" from deportation, but she could no longer protect her daughter. Of the 1,715 deportees on the October 23 train to Auschwitz, only 186 survived the war.[21]

Gerta was fourteen years old when she arrived in Auschwitz II (Birkenau). "Managing life in Auschwitz," she writes, "took a lot of luck, determination and newly obtained survival skills that one had to learn very quickly." At fourteen, Gerta was considered useful for labour even though she probably had typhus when she arrived. Only a few months earlier, the German authorities had murdered close to 400,000 Hungarian Jews in Auschwitz. Yet, the Germans had enormous labour demands. By the fall of 1944, they were moving slave labourers from large camps such as Auschwitz to other forced labour sites further west, away from the approaching Red Army. In the winter of 1944–1945, tens of thousands of prisoners walked or rode westward in open railcars. These movements of starved, sick

---

20 Lagus and Polák, *Město za mřížemi*, 243.
21 Lagus and Polák, *Město za mřížemi*, 271.

and exhausted people were known as death marches due to the large number of prisoners who died en route.[22]

Gerta and her fellow prisoners left Auschwitz on a death march on January 18, 1945, only nine days before the Soviets liberated the camp. They made their way on foot through the frozen landscape to the concentration camp Ravensbrück, about one hundred kilometres north of Berlin. Soon, Gerta and other women from Auschwitz were moved to the nearby Rechlin/Retzow labour camp.[23] Here, the already difficult conditions turned even more deadly as prisoners faced starvation, epidemics and frequent bombings of the nearby military airfield. Even during Nazi Germany's death throes, the danger did not subside. Thousands of weakened prisoners were at the mercy of guards who did not hesitate to force them on aimless marches well into April 1945. It was on one of these last marches, in early April 1945, that Soviet soldiers liberated Gerta and her fellow prisoners near the town of Neustrelitz. When the war ended on May 8, 1945, Gerta was fifteen years old. She returned to Prague in early June, making the almost five-hundred-kilometre trek from northern Germany to her hometown together with a group of young Jewish women from Slovakia.

The Holocaust in Slovakia played out somewhat differently from in the Protectorate of Bohemia and Moravia. Independent Slovakia, established on March 14, 1939, was deeply Catholic, nationalist and dependent on Nazi Germany, ideological commitments that quickly set the stage for discrimination and the dispossession of the country's Jews. Between March and October 1942, Slovak leaders consented to the deportation of about 57,000 Jews from Slovakia to Sobibor,

---

22 Doris L. Bergen, *War and Genocide: A Concise History of the Holocaust* (New York: Rowman and Littlefield Publishers, IN, 200), 227-229.

23 "Retzow (aka Rechlin)" in *The United States Holocaust Memorial Museum Encyclopedia of Camps and Ghettos, 1933–1945: Ghettos in German-Occupied Eastern Europe*, edited by Geoffrey P. Megargee (Bloomington: Indiana University Press, 2009), 1219–1220.

Majdanek and Auschwitz. Some managed to escape deportation by fleeing to Hungary. After these initial mass deportations, the Slovak leadership stalled and until August 1944, Jews were relatively safe in Slovakia. However, in August 1944, the Germans took control of their Slovak ally, crushing the uprising staged by local resistance movements. In October 1944, the Germans deported about half of the remaining Jews, about 12,600 people, from Slovakia to Auschwitz. Thus, Gerta's friends from the death march were young women who, like Gerta, had been sent to Auschwitz relatively late, a fact that probably helped them survive physically the terrifying last months of the war.

Paradoxically, although the majority of Slovakia's Jews had been deported to the German killing centres by the fall of 1942, the Slovak regime's subsequent hesitation and foot dragging vis-à-vis their German ally (unintentionally) allowed thousands of Jews to escape deportation by hiding, passing as non-Jews, or escaping to safety. Among the several thousand Jews who survived the war in hiding in Slovakia were Gerta's future husband and in-laws, the Solans.

When the war ended in 1945, Czechoslovak Jewry had been all but destroyed. In the former Protectorate of Bohemia and Moravia, fewer than 5,000 Jews had been able to evade deportation and remain there during the war. Half of them were Jews married to non-Jews, such as Gerta's uncle Franz who survived the war in Prague with his Catholic wife, Anny. They were joined by returning refugees and survivors, such as Gerta and her friends, who made their way home from camps across Central Europe. In the following years, almost 30,000 Jews emigrated from Czechoslovakia, leaving behind a community of about 20,000. The largest community was in Prague, but it had been diminished from its pre-war population of 35,000 to a mere 3,000 Jews, many of whom came from other parts of the country, including Slovakia.[24]

---

24 Lichtenstein, "Czechoslovakia," 122.

In the wake of the war, the new government was determined to reconstitute Czechoslovakia as a state for Czechs and Slovaks, devoid of the now unwanted pre-war minorities. This policy resulted in the expulsion of Czechoslovakia's ethnic German (who made up about 25 per cent of the population) and Hungarian citizens. Jews were not expelled but they were considered "foreigners," much like the despised Germans and Hungarians. The hostility toward Jews in the immediate post-war period, hostility that included violent riots in Slovakia, was fuelled by the fact that ordinary Czechs and Slovaks had benefitted materially from the dispossession and deportation of Jews. For the most part, Jews who decided to stay in Czechoslovakia after the war generally sought to integrate into society at large. They did so, for example, by changing their "Jewish" (often German-sounding) names to more Slavic ones. Someone whose last name was Altshul might change it to Aleš, or, as Gerta's in-laws did, Seidner to Solan. However, the fact that Jews felt that they needed to change their names also reflects the prevailing antisemitism of the post-war years, an antisemitism that made life uncomfortable for many Jews.

In 1948, after the Communist coup and establishment of the Communist regime in Czechoslovakia, Jewish community activities and religious life were severely circumscribed. As public displays of Jewish identity and religious practice were stigmatized, Jews relocated their cultural life to the private sphere where Jewish cultural and religious traditions could be cultivated among family and friends.[25] In those years, some Jews were eager to shed their Jewishness – something they considered a coincidence of birth rather than fate – and participate in the creation of a new socialist society. Others were less enthusiastic about the new order. What many shared was a desire to

----

25 For a study of Jewish life in Czechoslovakia in the post-war and Communist period, see Alena Heitlinger, *In the Shadows of the Holocaust and Communism: Czech and Slovak Jews Since 1945* (New York: Transaction Publishers, 2011).

rebuild their lives and enjoy the friends and families that they had. Much like Gerta and her husband, Paul, they lived intense social lives.

In the first few years of Communist rule, some Jews achieved prominent positions in the new political and administrative elite; however, this trend was curbed when the Communist Party initiated purges of Jews from its membership in the early 1950s.[26] Riding a wave of popular resentment toward Jews, fed by an intense state-sponsored anti-Jewish propaganda campaign, the authorities imprisoned and prosecuted communist leaders and bureaucrats "of Jewish origin." This witch-hunt culminated in the Slánský Trial of 1952, when fourteen high-ranking communists, including the former vice-chair of the party, Rudolf Slánský, were convicted of crimes against the state. Eleven of the fourteen were "of Jewish origin," a fact that was emphasized during the trial and in its aftermath. Many ordinary Jews felt the impact of the antisemitic campaign in their everyday lives, at work and in schools.[27] Jews, and many others who felt the hostility of the Communist regime, retreated into private life, focusing on making a living and on raising their families.

During this time, both Gerta and Paul were dismissed from their jobs, although Paul was able to work in a lesser position in his field of hotel management. Paul's "social" background – having wealthy parents – meant that he fell into the category of the "bourgeois." The Communist regime tried to "re-educate" people from such backgrounds by assigning them to do menial jobs, denying them education and otherwise creating obstacles in their professional lives. It was quite an achievement that Paul got to where he did even with his "bourgeois" baggage.

---

26 For a fascinating memoir about these years, see Heda Margolius-Kovály, *Under a Cruel Star: A Life in Prague, 1941–1968* (New York: Holmes & Meir Publishers, Inc, 1997).

27 The journalist and historian Petr Brod describes this vividly in Zusana Justman's documentary film about the Slánský Trial, *A Trial in Prague* (Ergo Media, USA, 2000).

By the 1960s, repression had eased somewhat. This new atmosphere allowed Gerta to work for the American company IBM in Czechoslovakia. The government-led reforms that began in the mid-1960s culminated in the Prague Spring, when Alexander Dubček, the country's leader, embarked on creating "socialism with a human face" by easing government control and allowing far-reaching individual freedoms. While Soviet and neighbouring Communist leaders had watched the reform movement with suspicion from the outset, they now feared that Czechoslovak policies would undo the socialist system there – and perhaps elsewhere. The Soviet Union and its allies invaded Czechoslovakia on August 21, 1968, and deposed the reform leadership. In the months that followed, when the authorities kept the borders open, thousands of Czechoslovaks left the country. More than 21,000 refugees from Czechoslovakia arrived in Canada between 1968 and 1969, among them the Solans.[28]

When Gerta, her husband, Paul, and their teenaged son, Michal, left Czechoslovakia for Canada, she left few relatives behind. Gerta Solan's story is one of many that reflect the destruction the Holocaust wrought on Jewish families in Europe. When World War II ended, survivors strove to restart their lives, often having to establish entirely new families, having lost their own. Over time, many Holocaust survivors, faced with either traumatic reminders of their past or ongoing antisemitism, decided to begin their lives yet again, far away from the place they had called home.

Tatjana Lichtenstein
The University of Texas at Austin
2014

---

28 For an overview of the different waves of immigrants and refugees coming to Canada from Czechoslovakia in the twentieth century, see "Czechs," in *Encyclopedia of Canada's Peoples*, edited by Paul Robert Magocsi (Toronto: University of Toronto Press, 1999), 397–405, here 400.

LEGEND

Borders 1921-1938

Borders 1939-1944

N

0   50   100km

Rechlin

Ravensbrück

Berlin

GERMANY

Elbe

Vistula

Warsaw

POLAND

Oder

Theresienstadt

Prague

Krakow

Auschwitz-Birkenau

C Z E C H O S L O V A K I A

Podmokly

Trenčín

Banská Bystrica

Danube

Vienna   Bratislava

AUSTRIA

Budapest

HUNGARY

I dedicate this memoir, with love, to my son, Michal, my grandsons, Yair and Daniel, and my granddaughter, Noya.

I also wish to express my gratitude to Grace Moffitt and Virginia Zinner, who helped with editing the first draft of my memoir.

Author's Preface

About fifty years after the end of World War II, well-known movie director Steven Spielberg started a project to preserve the stories of Holocaust survivors, donating the proceeds from his movie *Schindler's List* to support it. Teams of interviewers videotaped Holocaust survivors in countries around the world, carefully documenting all the information. [1]

A friend I met in Auschwitz and encountered again by chance in Toronto after the war tried to convince me how necessary it was to be interviewed. I thought about it for quite a few days and came to the conclusion that it was my duty to speak out for all the people who went through the horrors of Nazi suffering and didn't survive, as well as for our children and the next generation. It was not easy returning to these terrifying times, but it was necessary. My heart is now at ease and my soul is at peace, content to have contributed my experience toward such an important cause.

When I had a copy of my tape made for my son, Michal (Mishko), and sent it to him in Israel, he phoned me to say that it was the best

---

1 For information on Steven Spielberg, as well as on other significant people and historical events; historical, religious and cultural terms; major organizations; geographical locations; and foreign-language words and expressions contained in the text, please see the glossary.

thing he had ever seen. He valued the overwhelming amount of information I provided and told me how proud he was and that he loves me very much. That meant a lot to me, and will always warm my heart.

Out of the approximately 15,000 children who passed through the Theresienstadt camp, I was one of the 150 children to have survived. I have only written about part of my experiences in the concentration camps in this memoir. There have already been so many good books on this subject that I barely had the courage to add to them, but what I describe here are my feelings and personal memories of this tragic period of my life.

A Carefree Childhood

I remember my parents as extraordinary people, talented in different ways. My mother, Grete, played mandolin and piano and my father, Theodor (or Teddy), played the violin. Once a week, they held a chamber music evening in our home with their musician friends and I listened to them play for hours before going to bed. I started to play piano when I turned five and later on, when I got home from school, I would throw my books into the corner of my room and go straight to the piano, where I spent hours playing. It was one of my favourite entertainments. I especially loved playing "four hands" with my mother.

My parents entertained a lot and my mother was a gourmet cook and baker. She would let her imagination run, especially when preparing cold dishes. I remember one New Year's Eve when she produced a huge cold plate arranged in the shape of a clock with the hands showing five minutes to midnight. She could solve any crossword puzzle and she knitted beautiful sweaters and dresses. She was intelligent, well-read and handsome, possessing great charm and elegance. She had many admirers and her greatest was my father, who adored her.

After graduating from a business school course in Vienna, my mother took a secretarial position in an office there. Father was originally from Brno, the capital of Moravia in Czechoslovakia, but at the time he was studying in Vienna. I'm not sure how they met, but my parents' first date was on April 1, the Fool's Day. Notwithstanding the date, they fell in love and in 1928 they got married.

I don't know whose idea it was to move to Prague but they left Vienna to live there along with my mother's brother Paul. They rented a large apartment on Chrudimská Street in the Vinohrady district, where, on December 6, 1929, I was born. Later, they moved to the lovely old city, to an apartment at Křižovnická 3. I grew up in the heart of old Prague and loved the beauty of it.

My father was tall and well-built, with light brown wavy hair and sparkling blue eyes. He was good-natured most of the time, and enjoyed tennis, other sports and composing humorous rhymes. He was a business executive but also loved to work with tools and was an excellent handyman; he once installed a light in the glass cabinet where precious Rosenthal china was displayed and decorated the shelves with red silk cloth. One afternoon, my mother and I came home to find the coffee table legs in the living room shortened because it was the latest style. Father always dressed impeccably and I still visualize him in off-white flannel trousers. He was also extremely organized. When preparing for a trip, Father was the one who packed our luggage because, according to him, Mother couldn't do it well enough. He was meticulous.

When my parents were throwing a party, Father had extraordinary ideas on how to decorate the table. He would place cards next to the plate with a humorous rhyme about the guest. I could ask my father as many questions as I wanted. He was patient and glad to teach me about any subject. We took walks through parks, chatting all the way. He was the kindest and most cheerful person I knew.

My mother was always busy with various social activities. She usually took me along in the afternoons, which was quite exciting for me. I particularly loved a store on Národní Avenue called Pleta that sold fine, hand-knitted ladies' clothes. There was a small room in the back, filled with a pleasant atmosphere, where an instructor directed the ladies in knitting and crocheting, and tea and coffee were served with cookies. The next store, Veblová, a costume jewellery store, was where my mother liked to shop. My taste for elegant jewellery probably dates back to these times spent with my mother. After shopping, we would go to garden restaurants such as Café Savarin, or to Žofín Island on the Vltava River, where we met Mother's friends and their children. On Hybernská Street I loved to go with Mother to the Holland Mill, a Dutch coffee house on the second floor of a corner building that had a real mill attached to it. The waitresses wore Dutch costumes and they brought me a special mug of hot chocolate with whipped cream on top.

Mother was also friends with some famous movie stars, such as Gustav Fröhlich and Lída Baarová, who at one time was his wife. We once visited the Barrandov film studio, built in the early 1930s by the architect Havel, the father of Václav Havel, who was much later the president of Czechoslovakia. During our visit, Czech movie star Martin Frič was shooting a movie. We watched the actors and saw how they went over and over the same scene for hours. Gustav Fröhlich tried to convince my mother to let me take a screen test because he liked my personality and thought I would be terrific in front of the camera. Mother, however, was insistent that I have nothing to do with the movie world.

Once or twice a week my parents went out in the evenings to concerts or plays and on weekends to balls and parties. In the early evenings, when I was already in bed, I loved to watch my mother getting all dressed up. She was beautiful. One night, when my parents were going to a ball at the Austrian consulate, Mama wore an Austrian national holiday costume with a long plum-blue taffeta skirt and a white blouse with huge gathered sleeves and a black velvet vest over top. On her head she wore a flower wreath from which hung long red, blue and yellow ribbons, and her skirt was partly covered by a wonderfully embroidered apron. She won first prize for her costume that evening. The next day there was a picture of her with the consul in the newspapers, which I still have.

When my parents went out, my cousin Ella, who was twelve years older than me, babysat and we pretended to make cake dough for my doll. Ella had black hair that she wore in pageboy style and big black eyes. She was gentle and clever, and I liked her.

From family conversations, I gathered that Ella's mother had been a frivolous woman. She had had a child with another man, a daughter she named Edith. Unfortunately, both of Ella's parents died quite young. My grandparents took Ella into their home when she reached her teenage years, but Edith, who was younger, stayed in an orphanage. Ella attended a vocational school on our street and after graduation, she accepted a secretarial position with a Hungarian businessman named Lajos. Later, she became his life partner, though he must have been at least fifteen years older.

Mother was my grandparents', the Roubitscheks', only daughter, but she had five living brothers. Erwin was the eldest and after him was Hans, then my mother, Grete, then Franz (Franzl) and Paul, who was the youngest. As I mentioned, their other son, Ella's father – whom I never knew – died young. They were all born in Vienna and, aside from my parents and Paul, still lived there. I heard a lot about how my mother's brothers used to spoil her. On Sundays, they fought among themselves about who would take her out to the confectionery for coffee and traditional Viennese cake, or who would take her to the opera or a concert. My grandparents were of the poorer middle class and with six children, they could not afford too much. Usually the boys took in the opera from the "perch," standing under the high ceiling of the building with other students, as these were the cheapest tickets.

I was the only child of our family in Prague and, as such, I was my maternal grandparents' sweetheart. In their eyes, everything I did was terrific and I could always count on their support. When I skipped school, it was to the sanctuary of their household that I turned, where I was given love and affection.

Grandfather Friedrich, or Fritz, was very tall and still handsome in his seventies. In the past, he had worked for a branch of the Auergesellschaft company in Prague that produced the fishnet sockets for gas lamps. Later, they changed their production to electric bulbs. I don't know what position my grandfather had in this company, but I do remember that he travelled a lot. I also recall having heard that he was quite a womanizer.

When he was home, my grandfather used to take me for walks through the city, usually picking up some delicious sweets at the confectionery on our way home. My favourite pastry was the chocolate-covered ladyfingers that we bought at the store called Jiranek. The storeowner, a friendly elderly lady, knew us well and always welcomed us warmly.

I remember my maternal grandmother, Klara, as dear, loving and caring. She was the captain of the household, rushing from the kitchen to the pantry with her huge key ring in her apron, baking, cooking and having discussions with Maria, the maid, about shopping and keeping up the household. On a gloomy morning in 1934, when I was four years old, a near-tragedy struck my family. When my grandmother came out of her bedroom to check with Maria if everything was ready for breakfast, an unusual sweetish smell alarmed her. When she opened the bathroom door, my father right behind her, the strong smell of gas hit her and she saw my uncle Paul, her youngest son, lying unconscious on the floor, with the gas boiler on.

Why would handsome, twenty-six-year-old Paul have done such a foolish thing? It wasn't until much later that I learned that my grandparents had rejected his girlfriend of many years, Zdenka, a lovely, intelligent woman. She and Paul were very much in love, but she wasn't Jewish. My grandparents had tried to convince Paul to court Vilma, who lived in Vienna and was from a well-off Jewish family. Her parents owned a candy store in a "good" part of the city. Vilma was apparently kind and was willing to accept his marriage proposal and move to Prague.

My grandmother prayed that it wouldn't be too late for Paul to recover. The siren cut the morning's silence and the ambulance stopped in front of the house. In no time, the two ambulance attendants were taking Paul to the hospital. As the rest of the family crowded into the living room, my mother held my hand, asking her mother what was going on. Crying, Grandmother explained what Paul, who they called their "Bubi" (bubeleh) had done. Mother asked if she had called Zdenka and Grandmother answered that Teddy was going to do that.

I remember asking my mother if Uncle Paul would still make me the dollhouse, as he had promised. "Of course, my dear," she answered. "They will give him good medicine in the hospital and he will be all right soon and come back home. I will go to see him right away. You stay with Grandmother and I hope to bring good news." She was praying for it. Paul was the "baby" of the family. "If all goes well," she said, "we'll leave for Vienna tomorrow with Father, as we originally planned."

As soon as we got the news that Uncle Paul was recovering, my parents decided to undertake the planned trip to Vienna, so we made our way to the railway station. Mother, in her two-piece, beige-brown print dress, large straw hat with a band of material that matched her dress, and beige gloves, was extremely stylish and always drew people's attention. The funniest thing to me, however, was how upset she got when she saw a lady at the front of the Pullman car wearing a dress of the same print as hers. On that train trip we had dinner in the dining car and later went to our beds.

Aunt Anny and Uncle Franz were waiting for us at the Franz-Josef railway station. I liked them both very much and it was fun to be with them. I'm not sure if the fact that Anny was born to Catholic parents, farm owners in the mountains of Schneeberg fairly close to Vienna, was also an issue for my grandparents. I knew two of Anny's brothers, who, later on, were enthusiastic fans of Hitler, as were many other non-Jewish Austrians.

Anny was a special person. She was naturally clever and had a wonderful sense of humour. She and Franzl were sweet with each other, calling one another "Vogi" (birdie). Throughout her married life, Anny fully assimilated into our Jewish family, picking up all the original Yiddish expressions from Grandmother Klara and, as the years went by, becoming a real expert. Anny only had an elementary school education, but she had a sharp mind and learned things easily.

Anny and Franzl didn't have any children of their own and they both loved me very much. Uncle Franz used to spend hours playing with me and trying out his funny jokes, like pulling my ear and whistling as though my ear was whistling by itself. Even knowing his tricks, I was definitely the best candidate for a good laugh. We went to the Prater amusement park and wandered for hours, riding the Riesenrad, the Ferris wheel, that, to my eyes, was the biggest in the world and driving the bumper cars. We did our best to skillfully avoid a crash, though even if we did bump into each other it was fun. We also went to the famous Schönbrunn château and to the zoo. I never wanted to go home. But on our way back we always stopped at the famous Sacher Kaffeehaus to taste the delicious Sacher Torte, or went to the confectionery Aida and ordered hot chocolate with whipped cream and a divine piece of cake. It was only in the years after Hitler came to power that Franzl grew serious and distraught.

While we were in Vienna, we also visited my parents' friends and Father's sister Irma and her family. Irma was married to Josef Kantor, a lawyer who was president of the Chamber of Lawyers in Vienna. He was influential and did well financially. He wore pince-nez glasses and seemed not to know how to talk with little girls. My mother wasn't too fond of the Kantors – I think that she considered them snobbish. They lived in a beautiful villa and I heard that there was a round room there with doorknobs made of pure gold. In my mind, this family had a fortune.

When Hitler occupied Austria in 1938, the villa was confiscated and the whole family was allowed to leave for the United States. I remember their visit to us in Prague for a few days before they left Europe. At that time, their daughter, Lizzy, was sixteen and their son,

Quido, was twelve. I was eight. I clearly remember that when Quido and I were playing he started kissing me on the mouth, certainly my first experience of this kind.

Suddenly, we had to cut our Vienna trip short and return to Prague. Political circumstances that I wouldn't understand until much later forced us to return home quickly. It was July 25, 1934, and the Austrian chancellor, Engelbert Dollfuss, had just been assassinated.

Dollfuss had recently made an alliance with the Heimwehr (Austrian Home Defence Force) to resist Nazi efforts to undermine Austria's independence and its annexation to Germany. He had reportedly received arms and money from Mussolini and, at the same time that Hitler was gaining power in Germany, Dollfuss was granted special powers from President Miklas. In March 1933, Dollfuss suspended parliament, abolished free speech and freedom of the press, and dissolved the Communist Party and the Schutzbund, the armed defence wing of the Social Democratic Party. Dollfuss then formed a "rump parliament" known as the Fatherland's Front, that merged his previous Christian Social Party with other militant, right-wing factions.

The following year, workers in Vienna, led by the Social Democrats, protested against Heimwehr raids on their gathering places and the press and went on a general strike. Civil war broke out. After several days of fighting, Dollfuss, using the Heimwehr, crushed the strike, killing several hundred people, and banned the Social Democratic Party.

∼

When I was about six years old, my father's parents, Amalia and Sigmund Gelbkopf, celebrated their fiftieth wedding anniversary in Brno. We were a large family, scattered across many cities – and even across different countries – in Europe but everyone came to this special celebration. My father wrote a humorous newsletter, joking about family members and amusing situations in the past. He could be the funniest person on earth, entertaining people around the table for hours. I memorized a long poem to recite. At this reunion, I remember meeting my father's cousin Karl, who was a musician by profession and had come from Vienna.

In September 1936, I started elementary school in the building on our street that stood next to the vocational school. It was a special school for teachers in training where Grades 1 to 5 were taught. Since I was born in December, I was only accepted when I was six and nine months. I was curious about what school would be like. On my first day, I saw girls heading to the same building as I was, accompanied by their mothers. Our professor was Karel Fechtner, a tall, handsome, muscular man in his mid-forties who taught us every subject, including German. I was already fluent in German, so I got quite bored during this hour-long class. Nevertheless, he was a good teacher and the school had a high-level program. For some reason, we weren't permitted to speak German in front of the school, which I considered quite a nationalistic policy.

In the mornings, the last two-to-four rows in the classroom were filled by student teachers listening to the professor. In the afternoons, it was their turn to teach us and, later, they were evaluated by the professors. After a few days, we were taken to the movies, where we watched a film about animals in the jungle. I couldn't watch the huge snakes devouring each other; I closed my eyes and listened to the music. At that time I was quite taken by the melody of Schubert's "Unfinished Symphony." The music was so beautiful and I have loved this masterpiece ever since.

On September 14, 1937, Tomáš Garrigue Masaryk, the founder and first president of Czechoslovakia, died at his private estate in Lány near Prague. He was greatly loved by his people and was respected internationally, although he had made many enemies while he was in exile in World War 1 for advocating Czechoslovak independence from the Austro-Hungarian Empire. During his presidency the Czechoslovak people had called him *tatínek,* or Papa. A week after his death, on September 21, our whole school went to his funeral. It was my first real encounter with death. Everyone cried and was very sad. Somehow I understood that this was a turning point for our country and that life would not always be as sunny and cheerful as I thought it was.

Facing the Unknown

At the beginning of 1939, people, especially Jewish families, started to feel the strain of political changes. The Czech government of Emil Hácha was unable to prevent Slovakia's separation from the rest of the country that was encouraged by Hitler and the ensuing crisis. Slovakia's independence – led by Slovak premier Monsignor Jozef Tiso, albeit under German control – was declared on March 14, 1939. The very next day, German troops occupied the rest of Czechoslovakia and proclaimed it the German Protectorate of Bohemia and Moravia. The area of Carpatho-Ukraine also declared its independence from Czechoslovakia, but Hungary soon overran and annexed it.

The fall of Czechoslovakia signalled the definitive end of the political system put in place by the Treaty of Versailles at the end of World War I, weakened France and England, and isolated the Soviet Union. Germany was now the dominant power on the European continent. Soon after this, my parents decided to move out of my grandparents' place on Legerova Street and find an apartment just for the three of us. My mother found an apartment around the corner that she really fell in love with, but there was a catch – a German family was supposed to move into it. My mother, however, refused to see this as an obstacle. She made up her mind to go to the German Kommandantur on Bredovská Street and speak to the authorities about it. Father told her not to go, but she was determined. No one went there who didn't have to. I myself wonder why she went.

Inside the building, with Father waiting nervously outside, Mother was taken to see a German officer. They could be gallant, especially with charming ladies. She told us later that he had kissed her hand, offered her a seat and when she explained her problem, he responded with a handsome smile that there should be no problem in assigning her the apartment. Mother started to give him the information he requested, but he suddenly looked at her directly and, with raised eyebrows, asked her, "Are you Jewish?" As soon as she nodded yes, he got up from his swivel chair, looked at her with fury and yelled, "Raus!" (Out!), pointing his finger to the door. My mother didn't waste a second; she flew to the door, ran down the stairs and out into the street, took Father by the hand and said, "Run around the corner!" They were lucky to be safe and I guess Mother was happy to have gotten away that easily.

Mother found another beautiful apartment on the same street, on Platnéřská, next to and across from the City Hall buildings. The entrance was elegant, the stairs and walls covered with marble. The building had an elevator and our apartment on the fourth floor had wonderful stained glass windows. We moved in and I think that my parents were happy there.

Unfortunately, City Hall soon needed to expand and as we were the neighbouring building, we received a notice to move out. Our new apartment building on the corner of streets Dlouhá 19 and Rámová 1 was, it turned out, right across the street from where the writer Franz Kafka had lived about two decades earlier. Today, there is a memorial plaque on the house.

By the beginning of 1940, our situation had worsened drastically. Jews were only allowed to shop during certain hours and had an 8:00 p.m. curfew. We had to board the last compartment of the streetcar and we weren't allowed to attend theatres and movies or go to public parks. I could only play nearby in the old Jewish cemetery at Maiselova Street, where my friends and I jumped from one gravestone to another without any sentiment. We were just children who needed to be children. When I returned to this cemetery after the war, I spotted the large ancient gravestone of the well-known scholar Rabbi Loew right next to the entrance of the cemetery and then many others whose names were so familiar to me. There are twelve layers of graves there, one on top of the other. This was a piece of my past, my childhood. Sometimes even stones talk of sadness and human suffering. I took pictures of the stones and framed the photographs to hang on the wall in my living room.

Gradually, we were restricted from other aspects of regular life. That fall, Jewish children were expelled from Czech schools. There was one school for Jewish children right in the old Jewish quarter of the city but there were too many Jewish children in Prague to accommodate in that building. We had to take exams to be accepted and I was lucky to be one of the ones who made it in. There were still so many of us that we had to take turns going to class with another group of Jewish children. One group went to school for two months and for the other couple of months we did homework.

A year later, in September 1941, we were ordered to wear a yellow Jewish star on our dress or coat whenever we were outside. My mother liked to take advantage of her "Aryan" looks and didn't follow the restrictions for Jews. Sometimes she walked on the street without the star and came home after the curfew. Both Father and I got extremely nervous when she went out because if she had been caught, she could have been arrested and we might never see her again. We were also ordered to hand over all our valuables, such as gold and silver jewellery and watches, to the Gestapo. I remember lining up in front of the Gestapo building in Střešovice, on the outskirts of Prague, waiting for hours in the cold.

Far from our home, in the Strašnice district, the huge field that belonged to the Jewish Hagibor sports club was one of the only places where we could participate in all kinds of sports competitions and games. Close to my home, next to the only Jewish coffeehouse of Prague, was an exercise hall called Maccabi Hatzair where I met

Fredy Hirsch again. He was a twenty-year-old gymnastic teacher of German origin, a leader and trainer of Jewish youth I had known from Mrs. Friedlander's gym hall on Wenceslas Square. He was such a handsome young man, every girl's dream, although we were too young to know that he was homosexual. Everyone loved him and respected him. Led by Fredy, we participated in many wonderful games. My parents' friends still came every week in the afternoons to play chamber music, but had to be back home before curfew. I had a good voice and liked singing, and I was a member of the choir at the synagogue. It was one of the few activities I still did, along with playing piano every day, until the Nazis closed the synagogues.

In November 1941, Jewish families started to be deported to various camps, although we didn't know that then. There was nervousness in the air as Jewish people lost their homes. We helped friends and neighbours pack their things, sadly saying goodbye and wishing them good luck. It was the end of a carefree era and I felt the seriousness of the times.

Then, in June 1942, my parents and I were called up and we too had to leave our home. We marched out of our house with the allotted fifty kilograms in a knapsack and into a transport destined for Theresienstadt. The local baker, Mr. Matys, who lived on the corner opposite our apartment with his wife and six children, watched smugly with his big belly protruding as we left home for the unknown.

~

We were detained in the grounds of the Trade Fair Palace, where we slept on the floor. I helped out by taking care of the elderly; there was nothing else to do. I, like the other children, adapted to the situation, but we all felt the tension and were in no mood to play games. Three days later, we were taken by train to Theresienstadt, originally called Terezín, a small town that lies against a picturesque backdrop of the mountains of Central Bohemia, about an hour north of Prague at the confluence of the Elbe and Eger Rivers.

By the time we arrived, most of the original inhabitants of the small town of about 7,000 had been moved out to make way for a Jewish ghetto. As one transport after another arrived in town, every inch of space was used to the maximum to house people, but never for long. A Jewish Council of Elders had been established to report to the Nazi commandant. To meet the German quota demands for transporting Jews to "the East" so that there was room for new arrivals, the Elders had to choose who should go. Nevertheless, by September 1942, just three months after our arrival, Theresienstadt had just over 50,000 people packed into dormitories.

I was able to stay with my mother in the Hamburg barracks for women, but we were separated from Father for about a month. We were only allowed to see him when all the gentile Czechs had been evacuated from the town and the ghetto was opened as a family camp. Mother and I shared one bed in a small room occupied by four other women. One of them was in her early thirties and because she was German, from Berlin, she was allowed to receive a small food package from her relatives once a week. Her shelf was always full of sugar and other goodies. Hunger is a terrible ordeal and many times when I was alone in the room, I was tempted to try just a little bit of sugar or jam on my tongue to remember how it tasted. I never did, though; I knew it would be stealing. Perhaps I also realized that if I had tried it, I wouldn't have been able to stop.

Sometimes there was a "Do Not Enter" sign posted on the door to our small barracks. Even as children we were quite aware of what it meant and respected it. Inmates were still human beings with a need for love and sexual intimacy.

Father was eventually allowed to visit us in the evenings. He worked at the *Bauhof*, the lumberyard. Other inmates produced wooden soles, straw covers for military equipment and products made of mica, all of which were destined for the Eastern Front. Mother worked as an administrator in the *Raumwirtschaft*, the office that provided rooms for newcomers. Mother made soup for all of us on a small stove and at lunch time we lined up for meals with our military-style bowls. The food was sparse and not tasty. We were all very hungry, but I think that Father was starving. He was a tall man and had been strong, but now he had lost weight and his back slouched. It saddened me to see him like that.

Later I moved into the *Mädchenheim*, the girls' home. In every room there were wooden bunks stacked one over the other in layers of three. I had fun living among the children. During the afternoon, teachers stood in the middle of the room and taught us the high school curriculum. Whenever the person standing guard announced that a Nazi inspector was on his way, the books disappeared under mattresses and knitting took over. In the mornings, we were assigned to work in the gardens outside the ghetto. It was hard work carrying large cans full of water up the hill and watering the rows and rows of vegetables. Although it was exhausting, I still preferred to be in the fresh air. Sometimes we hid a small kohlrabi (a kind of cabbage that looks more like a turnip) or a few carrots from the gardens under our work pants to enjoy later that evening.

On our way back from work, we marched and sang, mostly songs by Czech composer Jaroslav Ježek with lyrics by our Czech national humourists Jiří Voskovec and Jan Werich. The songs were full of wit and optimism and people loved them. After dinner, we were allowed to walk in front of the girls' and boys' homes. We called it the *corso*, the promenade, as we indeed met the boys and sometimes had a date with one of them as we walked back and forth talking. We were hungry for a normal life we did not have, but in our little dreams, we tried to forget reality.

I also knew that Fredy Hirsch was in Theresienstadt. He had connections with the camp supervisors and had obtained permission to set up a sports field for the young prisoners on top of the wide, grassy fortress walls. I later learned that Fredy Hirsch was transported to Auschwitz on September 6, 1943, together with 5,000

Jewish families from Czechoslovakia and other prominent prisoners of Theresienstadt. Fredy and the children were incarcerated in the Czech "family camp" in Birkenau and he retained his position as elder of the children's block. On March 7, 1944, President Masaryk's birthdate, which was always a national holiday in Czechoslovakia, the children celebrated, but Fredy wasn't there, which was most unusual. He must have known that he and the children were heading for the gas chamber. I heard that he ended his life by taking Luminal.

Both sets of my grandparents were also in Theresienstadt, living in a house with many people crammed into one room. I loved my grandparents so much and my heart ached to see them in such difficult circumstances. My father's mother was so little and frail, but by then, no one looked good. Eventually, both my paternal grandparents passed away in the ghetto.

I occasionally stopped at my grandparents' house to bring them a few vegetables despite the risk of being caught by the Czech guard who probably would have imprisoned us. We knew and feared the guard, Mr. Janáček; whenever we spotted him in the booth, we got really afraid. Once, when I was returning from work in the gardens, I saw a familiar figure sitting on a bench. It looked like Grandpa Fritz and when I got closer, I saw that it was indeed him. He didn't see me. He had opened a small parcel and was hungrily eating something. I figured that it must have been one of the parcels we were allowed to receive twice a year from a relative and wondered why he wasn't sharing it with grandmother. I got angry, but soon my anger turned to sorrow and I started to quietly cry for both of them. My grandfather must have been starving. Nonetheless, in my deepest thoughts, I felt that he shouldn't have done it. I really did not understand his disloyalty.

I was only twelve years old when I was transported to Theresienstadt and it forced me to mature quickly, though my view and evaluation of the situation could never have been as refined as that of an adult. As time progressed and things went from bad to worse, my feelings became ambivalent, almost callous. Perhaps I was instinctively trying to survive an almost unbearable ordeal, one that never fades from memory.

One day in November 1943, an announcement was made that in three days an enumeration, like a census, would be carried out at a place called the *kotlina* (hollow) in Bohušovice, a large area about two kilometres away on the outskirts of the ghetto. Everyone who could walk had to be present. We stood for hours lined up in rows of ten while the SS counted us. Unfortunately, my Grandpa Fritz didn't reach his row quickly enough and the guard had to wait. A Nazi officer who saw what happened clearly decided to make a spectacle of an old man. He kicked him in the back and as Grandpa fell, the officer continued to kick him. If anyone had interfered, it would have ended in catastrophe, possibly in Grandpa's death. By then, my tall, strong grandpa was like a skeleton. He escaped with only bruises, but tragically, a month or so later, was deported with Grandmother Klara to Auschwitz.

There is a certain quality in most humans that helps them assess a critical situation in seconds and decide whether to rebel. My mother was standing next to me and saw the whole incident; it must have been incredibly difficult for her to control herself. I still feel pain and humiliation in my heart for my beloved mother. I believe that we must have had some kind of self-protective instinct against the deep pain in our souls. We had gotten used to seeing the corpses that were piled up every day in the funeral cart that was driven by a coachman leading two men in place of horses. Later in the day, the same cart was used to carry bread.

Miraculously, a cultural life still went on. Many prominent artists were imprisoned in Theresienstadt, including Czech composer and conductor Karel Ančerl and composer Pavel Haas. Both professionals and amateurs continued to practise classical music and an underground orchestra was formed in which my father, a violinist, was a member. In the fall of 1943, Hans Krása collaborated with the Czech playwright Adolf Hoffmeister in producing a children's opera called *Brundibár*. At the beginning, I participated as a member of the chorus, but after a couple of months I had to give up because I got hepatitis and was very ill. Lying on my bunk in the girls' home, I was weak and not allowed to eat the food we normally received. Every day I had to get a needle in my thigh, which was sore to the touch for many months.

Decades later, in 1996, *Brundibár* and other compositions were performed under the title "Lost Composers," at the Harbourfront Centre in Toronto.

At the end of 1943, to prepare for a visit from the Danish Red Cross, a major transformation began in the camp. Houses were repaired and painted; rose bushes were planted; a music pavilion was erected and children's playgrounds were built. Small shops were restored and signs such as "Grocery," "Bakery" and "Library" were placed above them; ghetto money was printed and used as the local currency; goods that had been confiscated from new arrivals were displayed in the shop windows. My grandmother found her old dress displayed in a store window and bought it, happy to have it back.

The agenda for the Red Cross visit was meticulously arranged. Dr. Eppstein, the chairman of the Council of Elders, wrote out answers to possible questions from the visitors in advance, submitting them to the Nazi authorities for approval. Everything that the visitors would see was carefully prepared, every point checked. Not one wayward incident would be tolerated.

The visit took place on a summer day in June 1944. I learned much later that the group was comprised of Franz Hvass from the Danish Foreign Office and Dr. E. Juel-Henningsen from the Danish Ministry of Health on behalf of the Danish Red Cross, as well as Maurice Rossel, deputy head of the International Red Cross, who worked in the Berlin office. There were fourteen visitors that day, including representatives from the German Red Cross and the German Foreign

Office, and SS officials from the Protectorate. That day, Dr. Eppstein, dubbed the "mayor," drove around with the delegation in a limousine, wearing a black suit and top hat. They made a stop at his office, which had been newly furnished with a carpet, where Eppstein outlined the ghetto's logistics to the visitors using pretend statistics.

From the morning until early evening, the guests witnessed a variety of staged events that likely had a casual appearance – smiling children, contented workers. They also saw a performance of the children's opera *Brundibár*. All the youngsters, me included, had been taken to a newly built *Kaffeehaus* on the main square, next to the SS Kommandantur and told to sit at the tables. They had put makeup on our faces. A piece of cake appeared in front of each one of us, which was tempting and we knew we would regret eating it. We enjoyed it for the moment, but later, indeed, I got very sick.

The Red Cross delegation did not see the conditions in the living quarters or the hospitals, nor did they see the deportation records, the dead, or the Czech guards. They only walked along the prepared route, impressed by what they saw. I read that in Dr. Rossel's report of the visit, he wondered why the Germans had postponed the visit for so long. After all, they had nothing at all to hide.

Shortly after the visit, inmates were forced to participate in the making of a Nazi propaganda film called *Theresienstadt: A Documentary Film from the Jewish Settlement Area*, which came to be referred to as "The Führer Gives the Jews a City." Well-known German-Jewish actor Kurt Gerron directed a production crew in cooperation with some Czech and Dutch artists. Karl Rahm, the camp's commandant, supervised the script. One evening after work, we were called to appear in a huge public bathroom in one of the barracks on the main square. I was told to undress and stay in my underwear, and was filmed washing my face and cleaning my teeth. My mother must have been worried, as we were not allowed to let our parents know where we were. Other people were filmed playing soccer and a concert took place under the baton of Karel Ančerl. This was done to counter any negative perceptions of how the Germans were treating us; they intended to show the world that the town was an exemplary settlement for Jews.

~

The summons to a transport always came suddenly and deportees were given only twenty-four hours to pack their belongings. My father got his summons some time in September 1944. The people selected for transport were held on the main floor of the Hamburg barracks, as directly behind the back gate was the railway siding with the prepared cattle wagons. For some unknown reason, and much to our delight, there was a delay of three days. Whenever we could, Mother and I went to see Father. On the fourth morning, however, he was gone.

Then, on October 23, 1944, it happened to me. I was assigned to a transport to go "East." My mother was alarmed and prepared to join me. I asked her not to, but she wouldn't listen and I must admit I was relieved not to have to face the "unknown" by myself. My mother was always very brave and before stepping into the cattle train, she addressed the commandant of the camp, Karl Rahm, who was standing nearby. She spoke German fluently and explained that she was voluntarily accompanying me and asked him to release me from the transport. He gave her a long stare, then pointed with his finger to the train and said, "Einsteigen, und schnell!" (Get on, quickly!)

The train was dark and cold and we only had pails to relieve ourselves. A few men and women died on the way. When the train stopped a couple of days later, the iron bars were removed from the door and we were told to step down. Orders were given to carry the corpses out and put them on the ground, next to the tracks. We had arrived in Auschwitz.

Surviving the Unbearable

SS men shouted at us to line up, yelling, "Go! Go! Go!" to move us forward. There was a huge factory chimney releasing thick smoke into the air. Some of the female inmates told us that people were being gassed, sometimes just lightly, before being thrown into ovens. There were bodies burning day and night. A barbed wire fence charged with electricity surrounded the camp. Later, a few times, I saw women jumping to embrace the wires, wanting to end their misery.

We were given summer clothing, each piece marked with a huge X on the back, socks and Dutch wooden shoes. It was October and the sky was grey, the wind strong; it was freezing cold. The inmates who were there already were unfriendly – I think they envied us arriving later than they had. The constant shouting of uniformed SS women accompanied by large dogs was terrifying. We knew we were facing a horrible fate. This was Birkenau, a death camp.

We were ordered to line up to be tattooed. On my inside left arm I was given the number A 27635. Less than a week later, we underwent one of the now well-known selections done by physicians like Dr. Mengele and Dr. König. I was very thin and undernourished and with one wave of the doctor's hand, my mother and I were separated. I saw my mother's desperate face trying to follow me, but she was pushed back. I was alone.

Like cattle we were pushed into trucks, hundreds of us heading to, I was sure, the gas chamber to end as dust in the chimney. They took us into a large room and told us to undress. It must have been late, as it was dark outside. Women started to scream hysterically that we were going to be gassed. We may have actually been in one of the delousing barracks, not the gas chambers at all, but I was in a daze and, as I remember it, I moved to a window. I looked around; no one was watching me. Everyone was in her own strange world of despair. I pushed my small head through an opening in the window, and then my shoulders and the rest of my body went through like butter. I didn't hear or see any dogs. I jumped down and ran. I had nothing to lose. I knew I had to get into a barracks. I found one and tried to get onto a bunk but they were all filled. It was pitch dark. In the middle of the barracks was something like a huge steam boiler. I climbed up on it to sit down. It was quiet. Suddenly, I got a terrible toothache. Then something heavy and alive fell on me and jumped away – rats!

Life started at 5:00 a.m. in the camps and the next morning I heard shouts from the block elders, ordering us to get out and line up for the *Appell*, the head count. I had survived the night, but I knew I had to go out and line up. I remember standing in line, stiff, freezing, but don't remember anything after that. I must have fainted.

I woke up on a top bunk in the hospital with another girl next to me. It was the least safe place to be because it was the first place they went to collect people to send to the gas chamber. But I was weak and couldn't go anywhere. When my neighbour saw that I had opened my eyes, she said, "You have probably survived typhus."

A woman doctor in the infirmary, an inmate originally from Brno, my father's hometown, helped me to avoid selection for the gas chamber by releasing me to the children's barracks at the right time. There were children there from two to fourteen years of age, as I was. The girl from the hospital was also there. She was my age, from Prague, and her name was Eva Stern. We played with the other, smaller children. It seemed to be a safe place. One day, when we went to shower I was alarmed at first because the room looked similar to the one I had been in that I thought was next to the gas chamber. But what came out of the showers was indeed water. It was warm and pleasant. What a luxury! Two SS women were watching us and one of them, pointing to my face, called to the other, "Look, she might have been pretty."

Eva and I were taken from the children's block to a place I thought was the city because there were red brick houses, but those might have been the quarters for other, more privileged labourers. Some officers took us to a munitions factory, along with a few other women who were picked up on the way. Directing us to a long table where women were making mechanical adjustments to ammunition, they put us to work. Every evening, we returned to the camp.

One evening, when we arrived at the camp after work, a dead, deformed body lay on the ground next to the gate, an SS officer kicking the body with his heavy boots until the belly slit open. We were all ordered to look at it. A warning to all the inmates, it was the body of a young woman who had been caught trying to escape. Without a chain of underground helpers, there was no chance of escape. As soon as it was discovered that an inmate was missing, the camp's sirens started to howl and guards with dogs were always able to find the escapee. All around the complex were a long chain of electric fences, watchtowers that were manned day and night, ditches, trained watchdogs and SS guards armed with machine guns. There was no civilian population within a forty-kilometre radius of the camp complex. The entire area was closed off, flat and exposed; any movement could be seen for miles.

Managing life in Auschwitz took a lot of luck, determination and newly obtained survival skills that one had to learn very quickly. There was corruption and there were thefts. Shoes of any kind and clothes were exchanged among prisoners for a piece of bread, a spoon of sugar, a pinch of salt. We had to hide these "valuables" under our bodies while sleeping at night.

We had no opportunity to maintain any semblance of cleanliness. From time to time we washed our shaven heads, the bristles slightly longer after a month, in the weak morning coffee ration they supplied, which was just brown water anyway. We didn't own a toothbrush or toothpaste – my teeth were covered with a light brown film the colour of chocolate. I once found a small piece of a broken mirror and looked into it, trying to smile at myself, but it was rather an ugly grimace. I was amazed how unattractive I had become.

Approximately twice a month we were taken to a barracks to shower. There was no toilet paper, nor any other paper. I used the lining of my jacket torn into small pieces. Serious skin infections were frequent, usually ignored, because no one wanted to risk seeing a doctor who might decide to gas you for being ill and skeletal. I got an infection called impetigo on my leg. It was highly infectious and practically ate a hole in my flesh. I was very lucky that it cleaned up by itself, although there was a visible mark on the spot for many years after.

We were forced to work in ammunition factories or stone mines under the watch of SS guards. Only the "privileged" prisoners or those who knew a trade worked in different departments. Some were doctors or nurses assisting the SS doctors, some sorted out clothing and items confiscated from prisoners on their arrival and others sorted out gold teeth and bridges taken from the mouths of prisoners who were killed or had not survived the harsh regime. There were special prisoners who worked in the crematoria and were forced to feed the ovens with bodies that had been gassed or killed otherwise. These workers were later gassed as well, for knowing too much.

One day after work, I came across a man and a woman lying together on the floor of the washroom vigorously engaged in a kind of rhythm, puffing and moaning. I watched them with horror and disgust. Intensely occupied with each other, they didn't take any notice of me. Both wore the striped uniforms of inmates. I thought he must have been a kapo (a foreman) because no other man would have dared enter the barracks. Confused and upset, I was unable to move; I wanted so much to be with my mother, but I had no idea where she was. The couple stopped their movements and he handed her a piece of bread. Then my feet responded to the brain's command to run away. I had nobody in this jungle of animals to talk to. I was silent for about a week.

The evenings, lying on our narrow bunks, six people side by side on each of three levels, were the most humane time of our life in the camp. Sometimes we sang well-known songs and listened to the voices of two sisters who sang beautifully in French. It reminded us of the normal life we so longed for.

The kapo and block elder had a quite cozy room at the entrance to the barracks, where they slept and worked during the day. In the evenings, it was incredibly difficult to suppress our hunger as they cooked their extra dinner, taken from our rations, on their little stove; the smell floated through the air directly into our nostrils. We promised each other that if we survived, we would never, ever in our lives go hungry again.

A woman in her early forties who shared my bunk was also from Prague and we sometimes talked about our families. One night she said, "If we survive and return home and you are alone, I will adopt you." We were living from one minute to the next and now I don't even remember her name. Maybe I never knew her family name.

I also played a game of nostalgia, recalling memories of the past to forget, for a while, the terrible present. The game was to specify a street in Prague, name one store after the other and list the merchandise they carried. We lulled ourselves to sleep with these dreams, our heads resting on our most valuable possessions – our wooden shoes wrapped into our jackets – both of which would otherwise have been stolen during the night. My dreams often led me into a wonderful, colourful cornfield mixed with flowers, lightly blowing from side to side in the wind. The siren at 5:00 a.m. woke us to the morning reality of roll call. We each wondered if we were going to be given another day of life.

One day, someone in the factory slipped a little piece of paper into my hand. The scribbled note told me to go around the corner to the washrooms and when I got there, I saw the figure of a man. This was dangerous – it was forbidden for a woman to meet a man. When he turned, however, I saw that it was Peter Eisenberg-Erben, a friend from Theresienstadt. We spoke hastily, quietly. He told me that my father, along with the whole transport, had been sent to the gas chamber on arrival. Peter brought me a little pot of soup; it was pure gold. He said that he would meet me again and would let me know when. I never heard from him again in the camp.

Auschwitz was liquidated on January 18, 1945. The Soviet front was moving closer every day but the Nazis delayed our liberation as long as they could. This was the beginning of the end for them. The very ill had to stay behind and later we were told that at the end they were all shot, but it wasn't true. The rest of us were dragged along with the SS officers running from the camp. I, along with Eva Stern and many others, started the long march across the country at night, slipping through villages so as few people as possible would see us. Some did spot us and tried to give us food, which was brave of them. Many inmates were unable to walk the long hours. It was the most exhausting race of our lives – for everyone a matter of life or death. We were weak, undernourished, miserable. People gave up and were shot when they sat down on the road, preferring death to such an unbearable struggle. Many times, I too thought of doing this, but some inner voice told me – no!

We went for days with nothing to eat but snow. I moved like a robot. Surprisingly, though, my feet continued to carry me forward. Then we arrived at a train in the middle of nowhere and were told to board cattle wagons on a train that took us through several railway stations. The wagons were dark, with just one small window in the ceiling. By listening to loudspeaker announcements, we tried to find out where we were. We heard the name Oranienburg, another concentration camp, but the camp was full and we had to move on. When the train finally stopped, we were at the Ravensbrück camp. There was the usual shouting and SS officers with dogs ordering us to line up and wait. There was no space here either, but they had to do something with us. By word of mouth, we heard that the gas chamber was no longer working. Perhaps shutting it down was a precaution of the Nazis as the war slowly came to an end. One female SS guard shouted that the young inmates should be put into the *Strafblock* (prison barracks), and that's where we went. People were sitting on the floor, leaning against each other's backs. There was nothing in the room – no beds, no furnace – just pails for people to relieve themselves.

Every inmate was identified by a number with a triangle next to it on the front of their clothing. Jews had a yellow triangle; political prisoners a red one; prostitutes – and other so-called asocials – a black one. Eva and I were surrounded by young Polish girls, but as soon as they saw by our yellow triangle that we were Jewish, they started to verbally abuse us with racist slang and insults. This made our stay there even worse.

A member of the female work commando that was in charge ordered us to carry the heavy pails of excrement outside and empty them. They were so full and so heavy that I could hardly walk. One of the SS women rushed after me shouting to do it quickly. The contents started splashing over my feet. I was traumatized but she was behind me with a whip shouting, "Faster, faster!" I couldn't go any faster. I was drained by fatigue and desperation. The excrement was all over my feet. The SS guard whipped my face and hands, and I fell.

I have no further recollection of anything in that camp. The next thing I remember was being back in the cattle train again. We ended up in the Mecklenburg area of Germany, in a small place called Rechlin (also known as Retzow). There was a small military airport nearby. We were hurried into the barracks, smaller quarters than before. Eva and I were on a top bunk, close to another top bunk near the window that was occupied by a Polish mother and her daughter, who was about nine years old. Under us were four Slovak girls, Eva and Věra, both from Trenčín, and two sisters also named Eva and Věra – we called the younger Věra "small Věra." There was a lot of bombing in this area so it was hardly a shelter for us. We looked up into the sky, wishing success to these brave men, hoping to be liberated soon.

Within a few days, a strange thing happened. We were lying on our cots when suddenly someone stormed into the room, yelling at us to get out because the Russian prisoner-of-war (POW) girls had broken into the bread storage and were throwing loaves out the window. We ran as never before because we were so terribly hungry. As I was standing under the window, one of the POW girls spotted me and threw a loaf of bread into my hands. A huge crowd of hungry women immediately shifted their interest to this one loaf that I was holding and tried to grab it. I was standing on a half-open cellar door and as the crowd pushed me down, my upper body started to shift into the cellar opening. Some of the women were sitting on my legs, which held me up and prevented me from falling into the cellar. At that moment, I wanted so much to live that I threw all the strength I had left into twisting my upper body around so that I could pull myself up onto the cellar door. I have no idea where that energy came from but I slowly managed to release my legs from under the women's bodies. I no longer had the bread but I was free. I felt hysterical – I started to cry uncontrollably and ran into the barracks. I probably cried for many other reasons too, and it took me a long time to calm down.

A second incident happened shortly after that. I was lying next to Eva Stern on our bunk and just as I started to get sleepy and shut my eyes I suddenly felt hands closing around my throat. I opened my eyes and saw that it was Eva. I stayed still, thinking that she wanted to embrace me, but she pressed harder and harder and I realized that she was trying to choke me. I tried to cry out but only managed a few grunts. The girls below heard me, though, and came up to help. They took me down and I stayed with them. I could no longer trust

Eva – I think something must have snapped in her brain. Such things happened, and no wonder. I didn't get close to her again; I was too afraid. The next day she left our room and I never saw her again. But I can still see her face, with her huge brown eyes, narrow face and short coal-black shaved hair, clearly before my eyes.

At the beginning of April, the Germans started to evacuate again and we were ordered to march still further. Some SS women changed into civilian clothes. The shooting sounded nearer and louder and we all thought that the front must now be very close. The Slovak girls were marching right next to me but small Věra soon started to give up. It looked as though she was going to faint. Her sister began to slap her face to get her going and we took turns giving her some support.

At dawn, we came to a huge barn, with horses, some civilians and some soldiers inside. We felt uneasy, but decided to spend the night there in the warm hay. Věra from Trenčín found a little package of soup powder. We managed to make a small fire and Věra prepared the soup in a small pot we had found along our way. She served small portions of the soup into the little bowls we had brought with us from the camp and we started to eat. I don't remember if it was all that good, but at the time we thought it the most delicious meal we had ever eaten. We sipped it slowly so that it would last as long as possible. Věra was still doing some little chores and I wondered why she hadn't started to eat. She must have been as hungry as we were. Then a terrible thing happened. I hadn't noticed Věra's bowl of soup next to me on the ground and accidentally pushed it over. The ground absorbed the liquid to the last drop. We all watched this disaster with fascination. I had already finished my soup, as had the others, so there was nothing to share with her. Věra stayed hungry and I was devastated. She didn't say one word but started to clean up the bowls. I thought to myself, dear, noble Věra played it cool, which she has done her whole life. We remained very close after the war.

We left the next morning and headed into the woods. Suddenly, we realized that there were no Germans around and that we were completely on our own. As we were starting to collect long pine branches to build a shelter for the night, all at once we were interrupted by the arrival of five or six soldiers on horses who were not in German uniform. When we heard them speaking Russian we grasped the fact that these were the Soviets, our liberators! We had never expected this moment to be so casual. We all spoke enough Russian to communicate, so we explained who we were and they took us under their wing. The Soviets love children and, looking as we did, they must have felt sorry for us. They took us into the nearby village of Neustrelitz, where we saw white flags flying on every house – the sign of truce. We were given food and accommodation. We could see that the German civilians were now afraid of their future and were willing to attend to our needs. We spent a few nights in one house, then moved into the neighbouring house, where we received warm meals. For bread rations, the soldiers told us to go to the Soviet headquarters.

The soldiers insisted that we have a drink of vodka because it absorbs heavy food and makes it more digestible. They were right – starting to eat normally right away could kill us. We later saw the tragic reality of this when a young woman who began to eat hungrily and couldn't stop died the next day. When I started asking some of the other people about my relatives, I heard someone say that she knew my cousin Ella and that she had died the same way.

There was a lovely Baroque castle in the village that had been looted by the Soviets and many valuable items were destroyed – paintings and upholstery were foolishly cut up and we saw wonderful china that had been dropped on the floor. When we heard that the Soviets were raping women, we knew that we had to hide the elder Věra, who was tall with beautiful, long, blond hair and had not been in the camps very long. The small Věra and I were so undernourished that we looked like children. I had been incarcerated the longest time of all the girls and weighed only twenty-six kilograms, a skeleton with a bloated belly, my head shaved. I doubted that any man would have thought of me as a woman.

We moved into the little gardener's house on the castle grounds, taking some essential cooking utensils, dishes and pots with us. The dishes were original Rosenthal china; we knew their value and enjoyed using them. For the next little while, we relaxed, sitting in the horse carriage, dreaming of our future. We needed the stillness of the place, the beauty of the flowers in the garden, the clouds wandering in the blue sky. We were afraid to face reality, afraid to find out which of our loved ones was no longer alive. We stayed there for a few weeks, but homesickness soon overwhelmed us and we decided to start our journey back to Czechoslovakia.

Going Home

Our journey home was challenging and took quite a long time. Every day, we tried to cover about thirty kilometres either on foot or by stopping military trucks for a ride; it was exhausting. We stopped, slept in German homes, were fed by German villagers. Then we met some Soviet soldiers who, although I have no idea why, were herding cows toward Berlin. We thought they could show us the right direction, so we made a deal to help tend the cattle and get them on their way. We had never done such a thing. I had always been a city girl, but we were all ready to learn. None of us knew what we were getting into and I soon got very tired. The soldiers were riding horses and I asked one of them to put me on a horse. He did, but the horse didn't have a saddle. It was all right for a short time, but I started to worry as the others were far ahead of me; I didn't want to lose them. I kicked the horse and he went into a gallop. This was definitely not good for my diarrhea, but at least I caught up with the others. I had only the set of underwear I was wearing, so I insisted that they get me down from that horse. After a short discussion, we admitted to ourselves that the soldiers had no better knowledge than us about how to reach Berlin. So we thanked them for their company and left.

After several more days of walking, we finally managed to reach Berlin. We stayed there for three days, each night a different family taking us into their home. Again, the Germans were afraid of their future and were quite willing to help us in every way. On the fourth day, we resumed our journey. We took trains, hitched rides and eventually we got to Podmokly, where there was a train that went directly to Prague. The train was packed and we couldn't get on, so we stood on a step right behind the engine with the sparks burning our dresses. We realized that we had to try to get into the wagon. When the train stopped, we finally managed to get in and later found a place to sit. We arrived at the main station in Prague on June 6, 1945.

Normal life was going on all around us, but we looked quite different and people knew right away who we were – we weren't the only ones they had seen returning home after the war. At the railway station, we had to go through a medical examination. The older Věra was diagnosed with typhus and immediately taken by ambulance to the hospital. The other girls went to a school where repatriates were accommodated before travelling to Slovakia. We parted and promised to remain friends forever; then I was alone.

People stared at me as I got on a streetcar. I didn't have to pay – I didn't have money anyway. I remembered the correct number of the streetcar to Vinohrady, where my grandparents had once lived in the same house as my aunt Anny and uncle Franz. Suddenly, I couldn't stand the stares of passengers any more and left the streetcar, preferring to walk. I walked and walked. I was now on familiar ground. I walked through a park, amazed that everyday life still went on: children were playing, mothers were talking. To me, the world suddenly seemed unreal. I felt overwhelmed with fear. Was I going to find anyone in my family?

Then I was standing in front of the house where my grandparents had lived. I looked for the family name on the board, hoping that my aunt and uncle would be listed, but I couldn't find their names. I knocked on the superintendent's door and when she opened it I saw a familiar face, but she, of course, did not and could not recognize me. When I told her who I was, she was moved to tears. She told me that the Roubitscheks had moved quite a few blocks farther north.

Relieved that I would find someone, I gave her a smile, thanked her and continued walking.

Finally, I stood in front of the right door and rang the bell. My cousin Edith opened the door, but she, too, didn't recognize me. She had also been in a concentration camp and must have come back ahead of me. When I told her who I was, she called my uncle's name loudly. He came to the entrance hall, looked at me in silence and tears began to stream down his face. He was unable to talk. My aunt came out and, as soon as she saw me, began crying too. We embraced and I felt such relief knowing that I was no longer absolutely alone. They were overwhelmed with joy to see me alive. I was at the end of my strength, though, and collapsed into a chair. We talked long into the night until exhaustion overpowered me. I had lice and scabies; my aunt bathed me with special medication to get rid of them.

I was ill for the next four weeks. I had a high fever and slipped into a light coma – the battle for life or death had begun. The family doctor didn't hold out much hope for my survival. Finally, however, one day I opened my eyes and the fever was gone. After that, I started to recover. I began to eat enormous quantities of food and gained a great deal of weight. I looked puffy, strange, but after a while I gradually stabilized my eating habits and returned to a normal, healthy weight.

But there were still many scars on my soul. In those days, there was no one to ask us how we felt or whether we needed any psychotherapy or other kind of support. It was better to block our past from our minds and face possibilities for the future. But every time the doorbell rang I jumped, hoping that by some miracle my mother would be standing there even though I had checked a survivors' list posted by the government. Her name wasn't on it. Someone once told me that my mother had been sent to Mauthausen, but I was never able to confirm that. I knew only that she was gone. I had heard my father's fate and I didn't expect him to return. I also didn't think it was possible that my maternal grandparents could have survived and later found out that my other relatives had also perished. I realized

I was lucky that my uncle and aunt had taken me in. They loved me and were very, very good to me.

My cousin Edith was nineteen, four years older than I. The first time in my life that I saw her was in the Theresienstadt ghetto, when my father pointed her out to me. Edith had a good figure, large brown eyes, a straight nose and nice teeth, and there was something about her that immediately attracted men to her. It took me almost a year to recuperate from the physical consequences of the war, but Edith was a thriving young woman and wanted to take everything in life that she thought she had missed. One weekend, we all went to the country and stayed in a cottage. I was resting in a swing net when something happened between me and Edith. I don't remember the details, but I do remember that when we didn't agree on a certain matter for some petty reason, Edith beat me up. I was shocked but I felt helpless. She was so much stronger than I was.

After a while, I just got used to her extreme behaviour. We argued but she never touched me again. I tolerated her because I realized that she might have been jealous of me because, considering her background, she had never had anyone who loved her.

My relatives in New York, my father's sister and family, sent an affidavit stating that I was a war orphan and I waited to be summoned for emigration to the United States. I owned a passport and kept it in my night table. Once, just out of curiosity, I opened it to check it out. With amazement, I stared at a visa from the Austrian authorities with a fairly new date stamp. I had never used the passport and it occurred to me that Edith must have misused it. That was a pretty serious matter and I gathered that she must have been involved in selling black market contraband, which at that time included things like cigarettes and saccharin. I didn't even want to think of the possibility that she could have been caught at the border trafficking, with my passport. When I approached her with my revelation, she admitted to having used the passport but asked me not to make such a big deal out of it.

After that, I felt that she was dangerous, without any scruples, and that I had to be cautious.

Edith changed men often and always seemed to choose the wealthy ones. Once she disappeared for a week with an older Hungarian guy who seemed to have money. They took a vacation in the Tatra mountains, staying in the best resort. Later I found out that I was missing two dresses, stockings and other accessories, which she had taken without asking me. Then she came home one day and introduced us to Dr. Rolland Černy, a neurologist. He was a tall, well-built man with black eyes, bushy eyebrows and a broad face. He must have been in his late thirties. He was crazy for Edith. Their relationship progressed quickly and resulted in marriage.

They immigrated to Austria, staying there for a couple of years, and then moved to Israel, where they lived in Tel Aviv and had a daughter, Ella, and a son, Ron. From mutual friends I heard that Rolland succeeded in building up a wealthy clientele in his private office. Edith was apparently enjoying her best years, playing tennis daily, flirting with her coaches and leading a full social life.

I met up with Edith again years later at Aunty Anny's funeral in Vienna. Even under those circumstances, she did not hesitate to ask me where I had gotten the Persian fur coat I was wearing. I was still living in Prague when I received a telegram from Rolland that Edith had died of a heart attack. I stayed in touch with Rolland. He was a kind man and there were the children, who were my niece and nephew. Ron became an engineer and Ella studied psychology, but later turned her cooking hobby into a profession, running a successful catering business.

~

When I was walking home one day, my eye caught the figure of a tall man ahead of me. He had wavy, light brown hair and broad shoulders; his walk was so familiar to me. Like my father's, his steps were long. I was afraid of losing sight of him and almost panicked. I told myself that anything can happen, he might have escaped death. After all, I did. I had to outrun this man, I had to see his face. I started running but when I got closer, I saw that his face was not my father's; the man was a stranger. My heart sank. It was such a collapse of sudden hope – what a gift it would have been to me to have been able to give him my love and heal his soul. We were not that lucky.

I knew I had to start leading a normal life and get an education. I also knew that it would not be easy concentrating on studies and finding my self-confidence. Yet, I believed that, having gotten through the last horrible years of war, I would be able to overcome any of life's obstacles.

The Post-war Years

My personal life started shaping up in 1946, when I got back in touch with some of my friends from the camps. Věra Szuesz (the older) had recovered from typhus and been discharged from the hospital. She was so lucky. Her mother had returned from a camp and was reunited with her in Prague. Together they returned to their hometown of Trenčín, Slovakia. The two sisters, Eva and small Věra, were reunited with their father and all three left for their home of Banská Bystrica in Slovakia. We all started to attend school. I was still not exactly certain what I wanted to do and registered for a course in an English institute on Národní Street. After the course, I enrolled in a private business school called Hlaváčová on Vinohradská Street.

I got an invitation from all three girls to visit them over the summer holidays, which I gladly accepted. I spent two wonderful weeks in Trenčín with Věra and then visited Eva and Věra in Banská Bystrica. I had fun with them but, more importantly, I met Paul Seidner again, a man whom I had briefly met before when Eva had visited Prague and invited me for dinner. About a dozen of us young people had gone out to a restaurant called U Patrona and Paul had been there with his girlfriend. When we saw each other again in Banská Bystrica, we had more opportunities to spend time together. I stayed there a little longer than I originally planned because Paul convinced me to wait and return with him to Prague, where we started to see each other almost every day. He was more than five years older than me and was mature, interesting and intelligent. Paul's father was a dentist and Paul was studying medicine.

During the war, Paul had hidden in Budapest and crossed the border between Hungary and Slovakia several times to escape being arrested by the Nazis. He eventually stayed in Budapest under false identity papers and even started to produce false papers for friends who were in danger. When the Soviet armies moved toward Czechoslovakia in the fall of 1944, the Slovak resistance had just mounted a revolt against their Nazi oppressors that culminated in the Slovak National Uprising of August 1944. The whole Seidner family, like many other families, went into hiding in the mountains, some joining the partisans to fight against the Nazis. Paul's family lived in bunkers for months and Paul and his father joined the Soviet Red Army until the end of the war, when everyone returned home. Soon after liberation, the family changed their last name to Solan, which sounded less Jewish. Many Jews who stayed in Europe did the same.

Paul's brother, Peter, who was five years younger, also came to Prague to study. Both brothers were influenced by their parents' dream for them to become medical doctors and enrolled in the Faculty of Medicine at Charles University. After a while, however, they reverted to their own interests. Paul was fluent in seven languages and soon pursued his interest in the hotel profession, starting in the Hotel Belvedere on Letenská Street. Peter, on the other hand, enrolled in the film program at the Academy of Performing Arts. Fortunately, their parents were well off and they were able to lead comfortable lives.

My relationship with Paul grew closer and we fell in love. It was a very joyous time for us. I joined his group of friends, who happily included me in their circle. We had great fun and were a bit naughty because we felt that we had to make up for the time we had lost during the war. On Friday evenings, friends gathered in Paul's bachelor apartment and we all cooked dinner together. One person made the

main dish, another made the salad and someone else made pastry, all
in a so-called tea kitchen, that is, a tiny alcove kitchen. We had dinner
there often, with about twelve people around a small, round table. We
also went dancing and to late movies, bars, theatres, parties and balls.

~

Amidst all the personal changes taking place in my life, there was a
political shift going on as well. In the May 1946 national elections,
the Communist Party of Czechoslovakia won and became the largest party in the National Assembly. Together with the Czechoslovak
National Socialist Party, they constituted a majority and Communist
party leader Klement Gottwald became the new premier. His government focused its policy on close and friendly relations with the Soviet
Union; the Soviet army equipped and trained the new Czechoslovak
army; and the government began nationalizing industries and redis-
tributing rural land.

In February 1948, a political crisis occurred – twelve ministers in
the coalition cabinet headed by Gottwald resigned, protesting the fact
that members of the Communist Party had been assigned to all the
top positions in the police. President Edvard Beneš waited four days
before acting on their resignations, but finally accepted them in the
face of political pressure and the threat of violence from Communist
factions. On February 25, 1948, a new cabinet dominated by representatives of the Communist Party was sworn in. The Western world
formally protested these political developments in Czechoslovakia,
seeing them as an effort by the Communist Party to establish a dictatorship. The new Gottwald government carried out purges in parliament, the courts, the legal profession, the army, the educational
system, the Slovak provincial government and the leadership of opposition political parties, including the Social Democrats, the second
largest in the country.

On March 10, 1948, foreign minister Jan Masaryk, the son of the
first president of Czechoslovakia, Tomáš G. Masaryk, and the only

prominent non-Communist in the Gottwald regime, fell to his death from a window in his apartment. The government officials pronounced his death a suicide, which still remains a controversy. Jan Masaryk was known as an intelligent, stable, well-educated, witty man, a joker who was well liked by the public. No one believed that his death was a suicide.

Two months after Masaryk's death, the parliament submitted a new draft constitution modelled on the constitution of the Soviet Union. It was soon approved in parliament without any opposition and Beneš resigned. Czechoslovakia was proclaimed to be a "people's democracy."

Although I was young, I enlisted, as did the majority of youngsters, in the Union of Czechoslovak Youth. We enthusiastically volunteered for different activities such as sorting out old bottles for other uses. We worked on landscaping to beautify the city; we harvested flax, potatoes and corn in the fields. After I turned twenty-five, I transferred to the Union of Czechoslovak Women, where I later became the secretary of a nearby branch. Our work focused on children's welfare and sometimes we hosted children from foreign countries. Once, we invited a group of children from France. We took them to a circus and to a performance of the *Nutcracker* ballet. Afterward, we invited them to a hotel dining room for an afternoon snack of open-faced sandwiches and pastries served with milk or cocoa. To our amazement, they asked for wine.

In 1947, I moved into Paul's apartment, which was quite unconventional and upset my aunt and uncle very much, but I just didn't care. I felt mature enough to decide how I should live my life. At that time, I was working in a store selling fabrics. Later on I got work in an office and was able to use my training from the business school.

I corresponded with Věra in Trenčín on a regular basis. She had written of her engagement to Laco Zeman, a pediatrician who was originally from the village Boshats near Trenčín. He was now living in Prague in a bachelor apartment near Wenceslas Square. She mentioned that she would be in Prague with her mother in a few days to visit and to arrange the wedding, which was to take place in a synagogue, as Věra's mother was religious. They also planned a civil marriage at the Old City Hall.

The day after their arrival, Paul and I visited them. Věra had turned into a gorgeous woman and her mother was tall and sophisticated. Věra introduced her fiancé, Laco, who was extremely handsome with dark eyes, dark hair and a wonderful smile. We took to each other right away. From that moment we all became close friends and visited each other or went out together at least once a week. We became inseparable. We met other friends and often we all played a card game called Canasta. In later years, we still played Canasta every week, with eight people at two tables, taking turns playing at each other's places. After Věra's and Laco's children were born – a boy named Jirka and a girl, Hana – we took the children out on weekends and in the evenings we visited mutual friends or went to the movies or the theatre.

While we were taking a stroll in Wenceslas Square one day, we met up with the Schönfelds, who were both from Banská Bystrica. Vilko, the son of the rabbi there, was a gynecologist who worked at a hospital in Prague on Londýnská Street. Paul had known his wife, Luci, from childhood. Blond, tall and lean, the woman was full of charm. She was a sculptor, very talented and intelligent, who spoke several languages. When we later became close friends, she told me that she had been jealous of me at first because when we parted she had asked Vilko why he hadn't said anything before about meeting such a young, beautiful woman. How typical from Luci. Vilko adored her, and they loved each other very much.

Around that same time, while I was waiting for the streetcar on Wenceslas Square, I saw a young man looking at me. It was Peter Erben – what a coincidence! He had survived; he was alive! I couldn't believe this was happening. We embraced and as we were talking, I felt, at times, that he was staring at me. By this time, I looked healthy and I knew he didn't see me as a kid anymore, but as a woman he was attracted to. I thought he looked muscular and handsome, with his large, brown eyes and intelligent, interesting face.

We went to a coffee house and couldn't stop talking. This was not a casual meeting – we were two people who knew each other from the past, had gone through hell, and were now meeting again. We asked each other about the time since we last met in Auschwitz with such eagerness, trying to absorb the years prior to the end of the war in sixty minutes. There was a bond of intimacy from having seen each other in the deepest humiliation of our young lives. We were unable to part; it was as if we didn't know how, as if we were in a trance.

My feelings for him lasted a week before I woke up. Peter wanted to marry me, but I wanted to return to Paul. Almost a quarter of a century later, we met again in Jerusalem, with both our families. There is an old Jewish saying that if two Jews meet and talk, in half an hour they will discover they are related. I had known that Peter lived in Jerusalem and that the best way to find him was to ask friends. Word would get around and someone would know him. And so it happened. Within three days, I was informed that Peter and his family lived in Ashkelon. We all met in Jerusalem next to the Tower of David in the Old City. His wife was a beautiful girl I had known from Theresienstadt. We had lunch together, talked and strolled through the city. Peter was an architect and they seemed to be well off, travelling through Europe and other parts of the world. When we parted, I knew that we had become strangers. That's life.

When Paul's parents, Jolana, or Joly, and Maximilian, who was called Miška, came from Banská Bystrica to visit Prague for a few days, Paul wanted them to meet me. We had lunch at a nice restaurant and I was nervous. They were very kind, but my instincts told me that his mother was old-fashioned and probably did not approve of a possible future daughter-in-law living with her son before the wedding. Nevertheless, as Paul was a spontaneous individual, one Saturday morning he suggested that we fly back to his home for the weekend. His parents were very hospitable and I think they liked me.

Around the end of 1948, my aunt Anny and Uncle Franz decided
to return to their home in Austria. They had always lived in Vienna
and Uncle Franz had an opportunity to get back the old job with an
electronics firm that he had had before the war. They both, of course,
took for granted that I would join them. We discussed it many times
and our opinions clashed strongly. Paul came up with the idea that I
stay with him, as our relationship would probably become strained if
we had little or no chance to see each other.

Though everything was ready for my departure – I had a valid
passport and visa for Austria – I didn't go. In February 1949, Paul and
I accompanied Anny and Franz to the railway station and gave them
our best for the trip and their new beginnings. I hated to part with
them; I loved them and knew that we would not be able to meet for
a long time because the Communist government in Czechoslovakia
didn't allow people to leave the country for the West, not even for a
visit.

Shortly after we said goodbye to Anny and Franz, Paul and I left
for Banská Bystrica. We got married on April 11, 1949. It was a small
wedding at City Hall with Paul's parents, his brother, Peter, and Geza
and Anica Seidner, his father's cousins, as witnesses. We stayed in
town for two months.

Before the war, Banská Bystrica had about 12,000 inhabitants.
After the war, when the nearby villages were amalgamated, the number had risen to about 20,000. They had a saying, "Alive in Banská
Bystrica, in heaven after death." It was indeed an attractive, picturesque town, lying in a basin at the foot of the Kremnica Mountains,
Great Fatra and Low Tatras. The town itself had both artistic and
historic memorials, the old castle district and the Slovak National
Uprising Square, with Horná and Dolná streets offering a lovely side
of an old, well-preserved small town with a rich, historic past.

My mother-in-law, Jolana, whom I started calling Mother, was one
of three daughters of a relatively well-off family who owned a textiles
store on the main square of a small town called Brezno. Her brother,
Bela, was a pharmacist who owned his own pharmacy and lived with

his family in a town called Žilina. One of Joly's sisters, Anca, lived in Košice with her family.

Mother was generous and genuine, always expressing herself candidly. Her household had to be impeccable. She walked through her large apartment in the house they owned in her neat apron, straightening out the Persian rugs' tassels with a special comb. Every week, like a ceremony, all the silver trays and dishes were laid out in the dining room and polished to a brilliance. The bathroom was large and one of the latest models, taken from a magazine, always shining to perfection. As important was the pantry. Dozens of jars of preserved jams and fruits were lined up like soldiers on shelves that were decorated with lace paper. On the bottom were five-litre cans, one with goose fat, the others with lard, as well as many other goodies. A family joke circulated through the years about Mother's reaction during the war when, before leaving their home to go into hiding, Paul wanted to open one of the jars of preserved peaches. With a serious face, Mother said hesitantly that the row would look incomplete with one jar missing. Everyone started laughing, wondering what the Nazis would think of such an inconsistency.

She had a maid, Růženka, who was also the superintendent for the other tenants in the house. Růženka had an apartment on the same floor that she shared with her husband, Jano, and her little son, Janko. The elder Jano was an alcoholic and little Janko was more or less raised by Růženka and Mother, whom he called "Mama." Our mother was generous to both of them and we loved little Janko.

My father-in-law, Miška, was a dentist and a wealthy, reputable man in town. Next to the house they lived in was a corner apartment building called Porgeska, which they owned and was at one time the highest building in town. Father was a well-travelled man. Mother had not joined him most of the time when Paul and Peter were growing up, although they had a maid and a nurse. Father was smart and we were fond of each other. Sometimes he chuckled over petty, old, traditional views. We once spent three weeks together in a spa in Karlovy Vary (previously known as Karlsbad) and we had a very good time going to the theatre, which had excellent repertoires, or to a cafe where a "five o'clock" dance took place. When some young men asked me to dance and I rejected them, Father told me, "Don't be stupid, have a good time."

While I was in Banská Bystrica, I took some Hungarian lessons with an elderly lady, as Hungarian was the language of the older generation and they understandably and automatically often changed from Slovak into Hungarian. I wanted to be able to understand them. Sometimes I helped Father in the office, learning how to prepare fillings and doing other tasks.

At home, around the lunch table, Paul's brother, Peter, often spoke about the pretty young girl he saw at Kremnička, a Slovak National Uprising monument visited by high school students. He was full of admiration about this girl, wondering how to approach her. Finally, he asked her out on a date. Peter was turning twenty and Maria was seventeen. Her parents lived in the nearby village of Podlavice and they were strict Catholics who would definitely not be enthusiastic about a Jewish boy. But Peter and Maria fell in love and were inseparable. Maria, whom we called Micka, became my sister-in-law and we grew very close. She is a terrific person.

When we returned to Prague, Paul got an excellent offer as a reception manager at the first-class Hotel Ambassador in the heart of the city on Wenceslas Square. He could not refuse such an opportunity. He also started a three-year correspondence course with the Hotel School Mariánské Lázně, in the famous spa town also known as Marienbad.

In December 1949, for my upcoming twentieth birthday, we had a home party with about fifteen people. We were living in a bachelor apartment, but the room was huge. Paul had the latest records, dance music of the 1940s. We all danced and had a wonderful evening; we were young and happy to be alive. When the last people left, at 2:00 a.m., I tidied up, washed the dishes with Paul and went to bed. We were still asleep at 10:00 a.m. when we heard the doorbell ring. It was a Sunday and we had no idea who it could be. When I opened the door, there was Mother with a smile on her face. "When my Gerti is celebrating her twentieth birthday," she said, "I have to personally wish her all the best." She was carrying a black sealskin jacket over her arm, a present for me. How glad I was to have cleaned up all the mess from last night! Mother would have gotten a shock at seeing such untidiness. It was so sweet of her to make such an effort and I appreciated it very much. It was wonderful to have her as a mother-in-law. After two pleasant days with her, she left to return home.

I very much wanted to have a child and was disappointed that we were not successful. Then the most terrible thing happened. I was home alone and, out of the blue, I got such a pain in my belly that I was unable to move. Crawling on my knees, I barely reached the phone to call Paul. From time to time I lost consciousness, which I continued in the ambulance that was taking me to the hospital. Paul was with me. At the hospital, the doctors diagnosed an ectopic pregnancy and had to operate instantly. I was bleeding internally, which was dangerous. Coming out of the anesthetic, I had not yet opened my eyes when I clearly heard somebody say, "Oh, she is a little Jewess." Not again, I thought. They had seen the tattoo on my arm. I ignored it.

The pain was bad but the reality of the situation was even worse – the surgeon told me that I should not even try to have a baby for two years. The first time Paul visited me, my face showed how unhappy I was. With a completely serious expression, he proclaimed that next time I shouldn't worry, he will put on his glasses and all will be fine. As painful as laughing was, I couldn't stop and already felt better. He had a dry kind of humour.

Another Difficult Political Era

In the early 1950s, a critical period of antisemitism was develop-
ing. The seriousness of this wave was the fact that it originated in
the highest places of government. In 1951, fourteen politicians and
leaders of the Czechoslovak Communist party, eleven of whom were
Jewish – including General Secretary Rudolf Slánský – were charged
with criminal acts of high treason, espionage, sabotage and betrayal
of military secrets. These were fabricated accusations of political ma-
noeuvre. The government had been pressured by the Soviets to orga-
nize a show trial in Prague, similar to the one that had been carried
out in Moscow against their own politicians.

The Soviet advisors and the Czechoslovak collaborators were
aware that Rudolf Slánský had a black mark against him. In 1936, the
Comintern in Moscow had sharply criticized Slánský for opportun-
ism and he was even excluded from the leadership of the Communist
Party in Czechoslovakia for six months. It took Klement Gottwald's
personal intervention to resolve the issue. At the end of 1951, the
Moscow security centre reported that there was a Czechoslovak conspiracy headed by Rudolf Slánský himself. He was incarcerated, in-
terrogated with other top politicians and accused of the above-men-
tioned crimes. The verdict of a death sentence was handed down in
November 1952. Eleven men were hanged, including Rudolf Slánský.

The long trial and verdict provoked hatred against Jews among both the public and the elite. Persecution toward Jewish professionals had risen in high places, resulting in their dismissal from executive jobs. Here we were again, in a dark era of antisemitism, in a new socialist regime. What an irony. The government, under directions from the Soviet Union, had to use whatever means they could to condemn those who were now considered "inconvenient."

Although Paul loved his work and was well known as one of the best professionals in the hotel business in Prague, he was dismissed during this wave of purging Jews from high positions. He had been successful in his job as manager at the Hotel Ambassador and had earned an executive position as general manager of the new Central Hotel Accommodation Service connected with the Central Travel Service, ČEDOK. Luckily, because of his professional knowledge, he was given back his old job as reception manager in Hotel Ambassador. Eventually, Paul got another offer as manager of accommodations in the best international hotel in Prague, Hotel Alcron. It was a wonderful promotion. Ninety-five percent of the guests at the Alcron were foreign, often popular politicians, famous movie stars and artists.

I got a job as a civil employee with the military prosecution as a court recorder in 1952. It was interesting work. I typed up proceedings of trials, which were confidential, and was surrounded by lawyers who were officers of the Czechoslovak army. Some were incredibly handsome and many times I was flattered to get attention from them.

The court and prosecution buildings were located close to the Hradčany district and Prague Castle in the middle of old Prague, overlooking the medieval towers of the city. Every hour I could hear the playing of the Loreta bells from the tower on Loreta Square. After work, we sometimes went to the old pubs for a snack and a glass of wine. During lunch hours we sat on benches in the terraced gardens, surrounded by Gothic chapels. In one way, I was so used to these surroundings, yet, deep in my mind, I was aware of the beauty and magic of the city, which was referred to many times as the "Golden City of a Thousand Spires."

Suddenly, I was not considered credible enough to work with confidential material. In addition to being Jewish, I also had an aunt and uncle living in the West, in Vienna, which discredited my loyalty to the regime. Every time I received a letter from them, I had to present it for censorship. I had been privately told by my highest superior to look for another job. With such political inhibitions it was difficult to be accepted for an office job, but with the help of good contacts I finally succeeded in getting hired for administrative work at a firm called Technomat, a big chain that carried electrical and household products distributed throughout the country.

We worked very hard and in our spare time, we liked reading. We read a lot. Paul was a quick reader and I, a slow one, because, if it is worthwhile and interesting, I sometimes read a chapter twice. I read anything that came into my hands from political authors like Marx, who wrote *Das Kapital*, as well as Engels and Kafka. We were members of a European Literature Club, collecting beautifully illustrated hardcover books by the masters, the best writers in the world. Our nation treasured books as the first source of learning and entertainment. I remember that when I was invited to birthday parties as a kid, my mother often bought children's books as gifts, which were generally considered to be wonderful presents. I myself loved to receive books for any occasion.

In the years after the war, we honestly believed that communism was a fair system for mankind. The theory behind it seemed good to us. As socialism developed slowly in Czechoslovakia, however, we found out that theory and practice are two different matters. There was as much corruption in high places as there was under any other regime. The working class was the leading class of the country and they were brainwashed by the doctrine of Leninism, as were some of the intelligentsia.

Under the resulting dictatorship, we started to feel oppressed, realizing that once again we were not free people. The border was guarded and closed off with an electrified barbed-wire fence. Only the "high society" was allowed to travel all over the world. Ordinary people received permission to travel to the neighbouring Eastern Bloc countries only. To go to the West we had to fill out a special questionnaire and if we were permitted to leave, at least one member of the family had to stay behind. The government was afraid that a large number of citizens would not return.

We had had to study the Russian language for a few years now, which was not a bad requirement – I loved to learn it – but it was hard to always be told what we could or could not do. Simply on principle, therefore, many people hated the Russian language. At work, we were told to attend meetings, which were mostly politically oriented, to inculcate all of us with Marxist ideas.

There was also a restriction on the apartment size for each person or family, with a certain number of square metres allotted. If the apartment extended beyond that, there was a monthly fine to pay on top of the rent, though it usually only applied to owners of the apartment building or privileged citizens. We regular citizens had to be squeezed into the regulated apartment size.

It is generally the case that the best jokes circulate under oppressive regimes. They pop up every day like mushrooms after rain. Jokes were heard at work, in the streets, on streetcars and at parties. The Czech and Slovak nations' black humour is well known, brilliantly expressed in the book *Dobrý voják Švejk* (*The Good Soldier Švejk*) by Jaroslav Hašek. The story is a satire on a soldier's experience in the Austro-Hungarian Empire during World War I. Beside Prague's large theatres, the city was also known for quite a number of small theatres with satirical repertoires that included hilarious political jokes. The audiences appreciated such entertainment and it was difficult to obtain tickets close to the performance. The artists often risked their future appearances on stage. Under communist rule, some were silenced or lost their jobs. People became afraid to speak their minds; it was dangerous to speak against the political system or praise the lifestyle of Western countries. An informant could make life unbearable.

Yet in a certain way, one got used to such a life. Human nature is adaptable. In small circles of friends or family one could relax and speak freely. One of Paul's colleagues brought to our attention the fact that the telephones might be bugged in some households, suggesting that we check it out. Indeed, by opening the receiver, we removed such an apparatus. We were nervous for quite a time after that, not knowing whether our future was in danger.

The Marxist-Leninist ideology also infiltrated the curriculum at schools. In some families, parents were hesitant to speak freely in front of their children, who innocently and unwittingly could have informed someone about contradictory political ideas at home. Also from a psychological point of view, we didn't wish to confuse the children by teaching them double standards.

Everyone at work was screened by obtaining information through neighbours, colleagues or other channels. The material was collected in a confidential file and locked up in a personnel office. Paul's background of having wealthy parents was a substantial obstacle in his career. Although he was recognized as one of the best professionals in the hotel field, he always had a secret agent at his back because he worked with guests from the West.

Not everything was bad in the socialist era. Child care was one of the priorities. There was complete health coverage for every person, although there were flaws in health services that could be found anywhere. One of the problems might have been low salaries for medical doctors and other personnel. In general, the standard of cultural life in large cities was still of a high quality. Prague was known throughout the world for the Spring International Music Festival, where high-level musicians from all over the globe came to play. Dozens of galleries and small and large theatres were well attended. Historical legacies were well preserved. Reasonable prices for beautifully illustrated hard-cover books, written by the best local and foreign authors, allowed all classes of people to have a high level of literacy.

∼

In early 1954, I was delighted to find out that I was pregnant. We were very much looking forward to having a baby. I felt healthy and strong, and worked until my eighth month. We exchanged our bachelor apartment for a modern two-bedroom apartment in the Vinohrady district. I did most of the packing, which I was always good at, and Paul just did the hard work of lifting heavy things.

On November 9, 1954, I woke up at 4:00 a.m. when my water broke and knew it was time to leave for the hospital. Paul took me in the car, but on the way we had to stop at the hotel to deposit some keys. After my medical examination I was told it was high time for me to get to the delivery room. In the meantime, someone called our good friend Vilko Schönfeld, a gynecologist, who rushed in. Everything went well and quickly. At ten minutes past nine, my son was born, long and healthy. We called him Michal, or Mišhko. He was beautiful, with dark brown eyes and dark brown hair. I was one of the happiest mothers on earth. Paul's mother came to give us a hand for about three weeks. She was a happy grandmother and even respected our rules for the baby. She was always good to me and we never had a disagreement. On the contrary, if a cloud appeared in our household, I always had her support.

Mišhko was a wonderful child – beautiful, active and bright, but stubborn. Stubbornness ran in the family and he was Paul's son. Paul bought a book called *Our Child*, which we studied seriously. We agreed that we wouldn't spoil our child, but instead would bring him up in a healthy way, introducing him to various sports, reading and other hobbies he would be inclined to like, and would give him a lot of love. In 1957, after three years at home with him, I returned to work and Mišhko went to kindergarten.

Our son developed into a beautiful young boy who was friendly and smiling most of the time. Naturally, he got all the infectious children's diseases, which was, in a way, better than getting them later at school. At school, he was different. He never gave any boy the first kick or push, but would return one right away. He was excellent in sports and, although he was intelligent and bright, he was not ambitious enough. He achieved only what he considered necessary to achieve. Sometimes he got in trouble with teachers because of this attitude. His black eyes were so expressive that he didn't have to say a word; he just gave the teacher a look of dissent. He was also a leader and without too much effort he sometimes led other boys into mischief, which eventually resulted in disciplinary warnings. After one serious discussion I had with his teacher and principal, they indicated that perhaps he was bored and suggested that he become a candidate for president of his class. He was elected.

～

One day, Paul came home and told me that one of their regular guests, a member of the team of executives from IBM headquarters in Vienna, had asked if he knew a good secretary based in Prague who was willing to travel throughout Czechoslovakia and report in person to headquarters in Vienna. Their professionals, who were from various countries in Europe, came to Prague, Bratislava and other cities on a regular basis to offer courses in computers. They needed someone who knew German and bookkeeping well, and had secretarial skills. The secretary would be dealing with government offices on the company's behalf, supplying employees arriving at airports around the country with currency, hotel reservations and tickets for cultural events, as well as making appointments with the representatives of export companies and arranging lunch or dinner reservations and menus.

Paul asked me if I would apply for the job. He suggested that besides being interesting work, the salary might be quite good. I didn't think that I had the qualifications for such a demanding job, which also required correspondence and conversation in German. The job description frightened me, as the list of tasks was endless. Luci and Paul were positive that I could manage such a job, though, and convinced me to apply.

Finally, I got the courage to make an appointment. I spoke confidently in German with a nice gentleman who would be my boss, and had to take some tests with his secretary from Vienna. I got the job! I couldn't believe it. I also got a large Tatraplan car for my own use and hired a chauffeur, Mr. Jaroslav Brabec. Only when my boss came to Prague did I have to let him have the car and driver. To my surprise, I managed to do the job and do it well. I dealt with a wide variety of issues and people and we worked hard, sometimes into the night. I loved the work and the salary was outstanding, as were the benefits.

One of my biggest assets was that through Paul I knew people in most of the hotels in Prague. The exclusive hotels always had a lot of foreign guests and it was not at all easy to obtain rooms but I had a preferential status in this regard, which helped a lot. When the IBM people were planning to have a workshop in Prague, I arranged reservations for their work space, their private rooms and the menus.

I was often offered an alcoholic drink before noon, which I always politely refused, but the waiter would serve it anyway. I couldn't afford to drink when working. So as soon as the waiter left the room I would pour it into a large garden pot with planted palms. I still wonder if they had a good time.

When I needed babysitting for Michal, I asked two wonderful elderly ladies in our building who adored him. We signed Mishko up at the sports hall Tyršův dům, which had an Olympic-sized swimming pool, and enrolled him in swimming lessons. He went there twice a day; Paul and I took turns accompanying him. He developed into an excellent swimmer, which later led him to the idea of training professionally. There was a special swim training high school for children with an interest in professional sports. The curriculum was demanding, with training before and after classes, and they required special entrance exams. Mishko got admitted.

In the spring of 1968, Paul's mother, who was on her own now since Father had, sadly, passed away about five years earlier, was visiting us for two weeks. During her visit, Paul called me at the office, his voice unusually alarmed because he had received a telephone call from school questioning Mishko's long absence from class. He had been sick with measles for two weeks, but after he recovered, we had sent him back to school. Or at least that is what we thought – we found out that he had skipped school for a week with another pal, going to movies and other amusements. On that occasion Paul broke our punishment rule and gave him a good beating. Mother was unhappy about the whole situation. When I came home and the three of us sat down to discuss the matter with him, Mishko admitted that he still felt weak after his illness, and was unable to participate in the heavy training. He was too competitive and was unable to cope with lagging behind his schoolmates, so he had decided to skip school instead. Paul and I attended a meeting with Mishko and the teacher. After a long conversation, the school was willing to take into consideration that Mishko admitted to having been wrong. There was a danger of him being expelled, but in the end he was allowed to continue classes.

Summer came and the children were preparing for training that consisted of a camping trip to Romania, Bulgaria and Hungary. They were all excited and looking forward to their trip. Paul and I took Mishko to the school buses parked in front of the school. As the bus drove off we waved as much as they did, but we could see that their thoughts were already on the road, imagining the adventure that lay ahead.

Uninvited Visitors

In the early morning of August 21, 1968, I was woken up by the phone ringing and sleepily opened my eyes and looked at the clock. It was 5:00 a.m. I picked up the receiver and heard the voice of Paul's colleague George from the Alcron Hotel saying that the Russians were here. I didn't understand what he was telling me. I thought it was a bad joke. George told me to open the window and look outside while he hung on. I saw tanks rolling down the streets, one after the other. Going back to the telephone, George told me that there had been a radio announcement about the Soviet army entering our territory.

It was first estimated that 175,000 troops invaded Czechoslovakia on that day, but later it was stated that this figure was probably an underestimation: it was closer to 200,000 to 250,000. By the end of the week, there were approximately 750,000 troops. The night before, the armed forces of five member states of the Warsaw Pact – the Soviet Union, Poland, East Germany, Hungary and Bulgaria – had invaded Czechoslovakia across four frontiers. In retrospect, it should have been no surprise that the invasion took place soon after the meetings between the Soviet and Czechoslovak leadership at Čierna nad Tisou on July 29 and Bratislava on August 3, 1968. Despite the Czechoslovak leaders' promise to roll back some of its reforms, the Soviets remained unconvinced of their commitment to Marxist-Leninist principles.

When the invasion started, Paul was away at a convention in

Marienbad and Miŝhko was on his school camping trip. I was alone. I had colleagues from I B M in Germany and the United States staying in the Hotel Alcron and decided that I had to get in touch with them immediately. I dressed quickly and went into the streets. There were tanks everywhere. When I got to the hotel, my colleagues were already packed, prepared to go home. It was questionable whether the airport would be open for civilians. Only one of my colleagues, Mr. Kobiakoff from Vienna, delayed his return until the following day. He was of Russian origin and had immigrated to Vienna years before.

We walked to Wenceslas Square, which was packed with both tanks and people who were discussing the situation in Russian with the soldiers, asking why they were in our country. Our people argued that it was wrong, that they had no right to be there. The Soviet soldiers were young and seemed to have no idea why they were there, or even where they were. They were given the command and that was it. They listened to the crowd telling them with bitterness that over twenty years ago their fathers had been our liberators, and now they were our occupiers.

Many of us spoke at least a little Russian and told the soldiers to go home, that they were not welcome in our country. The soldiers eventually grew impatient and the discussions started to heat up. The situation got serious when one soldier pointed his submachine gun at a protester and pulled the trigger. The man fell to the sidewalk without any sign of life. Other soldiers fired on the people, sometimes injuring them fatally. On that first day, the Soviet commander prohibited ambulances from being sent out to attend to the wounded or dead. People were angry and the opposition grew stronger. The streets started to become dangerous with Soviet soldiers on tanks and soldiers running around with machine guns. I couldn't leave the hotel to go home and I had to stay overnight. I got a room but didn't really sleep because of the continual sound of gunshots.

In the morning I decided to go to the railway station, which was fairly close, and try to take a train to Marienbad. When I neared the station I saw it fully guarded by Soviet soldiers armed with machine guns. It was impossible to get through. I took refuge with the Zemans, who lived quite close by. I was lucky that they were home. I knew that if Paul got back to Prague, he would try to locate me either at home or at the Zemans' place. I had no idea how to get in touch with Mishko.

The monument of Saint Wenceslas at the top of the square became the area where people assembled, trying to draw strength from each other in such a dreadful, helpless situation. The steps surrounding the monument were decorated with flowers and photographs of the dozens of people who had been killed. Some people who knew how to use ham radio volunteered to try to get messages through to anywhere outside Prague to tell relatives and friends who was alive and who was missing.

How glad I was when Paul arrived at the Zemans the next day! In spite of the heavy shelling, we tried to go home. Here and there were barricades that we could hide behind until the shelling stopped. Finally, we safely reached home.

Within two days, the chaos in the streets silenced. We were very worried about Mishko but tried to do our normal work. We had no idea in which country the school was camped at that time and decided for the time being just to wait. Paul, active and smart as he always was, went to the passport office and asked for valid passports for us all, as well as visas to Austria. He spoke fluent Russian. He completely surprised the Soviet soldier, convincing him of the necessity to enter. Paul came home with both the passports and the visas.

Paul took holiday leave from the hotel. I packed our most important clothes along with our documents. All of this had to be done in secrecy. We had no idea if we would reach our destination, but we had to try. If we were able to get to Vienna, I knew that I might be able to locate Mishko through the IBM office. It was still dawn when we loaded our car and headed for Slovakia. We knew the way so well, we could have reached it blindfolded. On the outskirts of Prague, the soldiers took the film from our camera but, luckily, they let us leave.

I was trembling. It was our first test in trying to leave the country – I didn't even have time to get nostalgic about leaving our home.

We seemed to have slipped through our neighbourhood unnoticed. Only the Zemans, two other close friends and the Schönfelds knew of our intentions. The day before, I had met with Luci on the street. We embraced and kissed. They were headed for Vienna and would stop at my uncle's place; they were intending to go on to Israel, where Vilko's brother was.

Prague was close to 600 kilometres from Banská Bystrica. In spite of having travelled that way so often in the past, we soon found it confusing because all the direction signs had been misplaced or turned in the opposite direction. This had been done as a protest by our heroically patriotic and creative youth, who were making life as difficult as possible for our occupiers. We stopped along the way and called Paul's brother, Peter, and his wife, Micka, in Bratislava, asking them to meet us at Mother's home. When we all got there, we let them know about our plans. We used all our skills of diplomacy to convince them of the dark era we saw coming and we begged them to leave with us.

Peter had graduated from the Prague Film Academy in 1953 and started his career as a director with three documentary movies. In 1956, Peter left documentaries for dramatic and satirical movies, later working on movies for television. Many of his movies were based on screenplays by Peter Karvaš, a well-known Slovak writer who was a lifelong friend of the family.

Under communism, there was a long period of literary censorship and oppression of the press. In June 1968 many intellectuals had signed a petition against the suppression of artistic freedom called "Two Thousand Words." Peter's signature on this document, together with those of other artists, meant years of silence for them. They were denied their best years of artistic work and prohibited from participating in their profession.

A high official in Banská Bystrica was in Paul's debt because Paul had once obtained a vitally important medication for him and Paul was not shy about asking him for passports and visas to Austria for the whole family. Paul had received them, so it was then their decision to make. Mother was afraid to leave her prominent position in town. She was used to a good life and we were unable to promise her that if she left. Peter wasn't willing to leave either. He said that not everyone could leave – he was an artist who had to share the experience of living through the situation that so many other people were in – and Micka didn't want to leave her large family.

We didn't have much time and had to say our goodbyes. We didn't know when we would see each other again, which was very difficult. We gave some people a lift part of the way – these were people who didn't have passports or visas; they got out of our car close to the border and walked the rest of the way.

We arrived safely in Vienna and stayed with Uncle Franz. The next morning, I went to IBM headquarters and on the way, I thought about my project for them. I had been assigned to represent them at the Brno trade fair, but after the Soviet occupation, I had asked to be replaced, telling them that I was sick. Going up the steps, I started to grin, thinking about their faces when I stormed in. I was right. When I opened the door, three of my colleagues opened their mouths and stared, asking me what I was doing there. As I started explaining what had happened, other colleagues, hearing the commotion, came in from nearby offices. Everyone was very compassionate, asking how they could help us. My boss assured me of any assistance he could give.

They sent out faxes and phoned their offices in Bulgaria, Hungary and Romania trying to trace Michal Solan. We waited impatiently for any results to come in. It was possible that we would have to wait longer for a response than the validation date on our visas allowed us to stay. The executives of IBM went to such lengths on my behalf that I received a medical record stating that I had had a heart attack and requesting a longer period of recuperation in Vienna.

The uncertainty of the political mood infiltrated other countries of the Eastern Bloc. There must have also been confusion in those parts of Europe. The IBM people told us that they couldn't locate Mishko anywhere. That did it. I told Paul that whatever might happen, we had to return home because it would be a catastrophe if the school decided to return sooner and Mishko didn't find us there. Paul agreed and we returned, waiting to hear from Mishko. In the meantime, I had time to repack and rearrange our luggage, selecting our best clothing and valuable possessions, including important documents.

A few days later we received a call from Uncle Franz in Vienna. There was a pause while he handed someone the receiver – it was Mishko! This was most unexpected. The school had arrived in Vienna and Mishko asked me what he should do. I told him to return to Prague with the school. The memory of families being separated during war was always in the back of my mind and I was terrified of that happening. The border of Czechoslovakia could have closed at any time and we couldn't take the risk. Our plan was to leave a second time, but only if we could do it as a complete family.

When Mishko arrived, we showed him Wenceslas Square and other parts of the city with tanks and Soviet soldiers. We tried to explain the situation to him and made him aware of our future intentions. It was important for us that he fully understood the consequences of leaving our home and our decision to immigrate to a free world.

Culture Shock

On September 26, 1968, we visited Mother and Peter to say farewell for a second time, then headed toward the Austrian border in our Saab, which was loaded to the top. My heart beat like crazy. I got emotional, realizing that this was it – we were leaving for good, trying to make a new life. We crossed the border without any problems and arrived slowly at customs on the Austrian side. We showed our passports; mine was a business passport. The officer returned a few seconds later and told us that my visas were expired. I froze. He returned into the small customs' building and emerged in another five minutes, saying that because I was an employee of IBM in Vienna, there was no problem if we stopped on our way at the police station in a small town to obtain a new visa. We realized that he had checked who we were on their computer and that our way into the world was open.

After driving two kilometres on the Austrian side of the border, Paul stopped the car on the shoulder of the highway and we looked at each other. We had made it. We had mixed feelings of freedom, uncertainty and apprehension about what would come next. Paul opened one of the glove compartments, and, fishing much deeper than usual, removed a heavy bag and asked me to open it. It contained our gold jewellery, precious coins and foreign banknotes. Paul knew that I would have been too nervous if I had known it was there – it was forbidden to take these things out of Czechoslovakia.

We called Uncle Franz, letting him know that we would see him fairly soon. When we reached the next small town, we went to the police station and got the visas without any problem. Coming out of the police station, I saw a familiar face. It was Stefan Lucky, a friend and renowned composer from Prague who had won a film award for his music. With him was a much younger woman. Isn't the world small? The first person we met outside of Czechoslovakia was a friend of ours. We embraced, surprised at such a coincidence. He introduced us to Mila, whom we knew of, but had never met. Stefan and Mila were not certain whether they would stay or return to Czechoslovakia. He was not young anymore, so it would be difficult for him to start trying to establish himself again in the West. We wished them good luck and continued on our way to Vienna.

We soon arrived in the familiar and comforting surroundings of my uncle's home. Uncle Franz had a housemaid, also named Gerti, whom we knew well. Their welcome was sincere and we felt reassured, yet we were anxious about our future, searching for answers, trying to make wise decisions. It was definitely an advantage to know the city well. We met friends at the immigration office who were in the same position as we were and saw people from home we never expected to meet under those circumstances: Professor Küerti, chief surgeon of the tuberculosis clinic in the Tatra Mountains, with his wife and their little dog; Judith and George Schanzer from Zvolen, a town near Banská Bystrica, who had moved to Brno; and many other people we knew. We discussed the possibilities, the political pros and cons of countries to which we might immigrate.

There were also representatives from Israel who were trying to recruit Jewish immigrants. Some people did decide to go to the "promised land," but we were not attracted to this opportunity. Some Holocaust survivors thought that it would be easier to apply for reparations from the German government if they stayed in Europe. Survivors could qualify to receive a high lump sum as indemnification from the government and possibly, further down the road, a pension. Even though I had been an employee of IBM Vienna and knew that they would have given me a transfer to any city in Germany, I strongly opposed this idea. We were hesitant about staying in Europe. We saw more opportunities for us on the American continent.

Paul had an uncle who had lived in Sydney, Australia for many years and wanted us to join him, but we were discouraged by the distance when we thought of how difficult it would be for Mother to visit us there. Paul had another uncle in New York, but Michal was the reason we dismissed that, afraid that he might be drafted into the US army during the Vietnam War. Canada, on the other hand, seemed like a peaceful country and we started seriously looking at it. We went to the Canadian consulate to inquire and made an application. We were accepted and within six weeks we were sitting at the airport, waiting to board an airplane for Toronto.

We had a lot of luggage, as Peter and Micka had driven to Vienna with many of our household items. Paul knew the director of Austrian Airlines at the airport, who was instrumental in forwarding our luggage without charging us overweight fees. He also arranged first-class seating for us. Paul asked him for the same favour for his friends the Acs – Pišta, from Zvolen, his wife, Irena, and their two daughters Katka and Mirka. They sat next to us. There were other families originally from Czechoslovakia, like the large Sermer family of three brothers and their families, whom we befriended later on.

We landed at Toronto International Airport on October 24, 1968. With the time change, for us it was already 1:00 a.m. We had no idea where to go next. It was a little frightening, although the immigration formalities were easy. Thanks to Prime Minister Pierre Trudeau, who granted Czechoslovakians political asylum, we arrived in Canada as landed immigrants. At the time, we had no idea what an advantage it really was.

Our old friend Věra Szuësz-Gold (small Věra) was waiting for us. For many years after, the story was told that after seeing luggage, luggage and still more luggage, the Solan family finally followed. Well, it was all thanks to the director of Austrian Airlines. Later on, our Saab arrived by ship, thanks to Paul's ability to wade through all the necessary paperwork.

Věra drove us to the hotel we were assigned to, the Ford Hotel at Bay and Dundas, and said that she would see us the next day. We waited in the lobby for another two hours to get a room and finally went to the room on the top floor. When we opened the door, we saw something that looked like two cells joined in the centre by a simple shower stall. There were bars on the small windows, the paint was peeling off the walls and the miniature basin was rusty and dirty. I had never seen anything like it. It was quite depressing. Well, we were immigrants, so no complaints. It must have been a "one-hour hotel." The women I saw in the corridor, wearing heavy make-up and dressed in a certain type of clothes, convinced me that I was right. Miško was almost fourteen and I felt a little silly about accompanying him to the door of the washroom. In spite of our tiredness and low spirits, Paul burst out laughing when he found out about my worries concerning Miško.

The next morning was cool and windy. We had breakfast in a small snack bar outside the hotel and then took a walk through Chinatown. We couldn't believe our eyes. It was a world we had never seen before. Little vegetable stores, stores with windows where ducks hung on hooks, grease dripping down, and dirty sidewalks full of garbage. It was dismal. We didn't talk, didn't discuss our feelings. We knew that we were all having the same thoughts.

Věra later took us for a short drive and showed us where to buy cheap household items. Then she drove us and our friend Pišta, who now went by Steve, to her home on Chiltern Hill, an area where many wealthy Jews lived. Steve was from a well-off family and had a great sense of humour. He had graduated from law school but was persecuted so much under the Communist regime that he was not able to practise and had ended up operating a crane on building sites. To us, Věra and her husband, Karol's, home was a dream and I wondered whether we would ever be able to afford that kind of luxury. Nevertheless, it was important for the time being that the three of us were together; we knew that we would work hard to achieve the best we could. In retrospect, we were optimistic. Without that, we couldn't have made it. We weren't so brave all the time. I just cried where no one could see me.

The next day, we all had to appear at Manpower, the government department that dealt with employment and job training, and wait for hours to speak to a counsellor. Paul's English was so good that he volunteered to translate from English to Czech or Slovak for other people. When my turn came to talk to the counsellor, I managed to communicate in English so well that he decided I should enter the workforce rather than receive an English course like everyone else.

Every day, in order to save a quarter, we made a marathon walk through the city instead of using Toronto public transit, the TTC. We only took public transportation if we had an appointment somewhere. We went by streetcar with the Acs to look for an apartment in the west end of the city. I was the last to get off and they all left the streetcar deeply involved in a discussion. The door closed behind them and I didn't know how the doors opened. Fortunately, some other passengers showed me that standing on the step opened the door. I thought that I would be left in the streetcar and would be completely lost. Doing things together kept us sane.

Shopping in the supermarket took us twice as long as anyone else. We walked through the store with a dictionary in hand to understand all the unknown products, but even so choosing the right dinner was difficult. We once bought a can of cat food by mistake. A puzzle to me was the sign saying "hot dogs." Was it really meat made from dogs? There were so many differences between Europe and North America. For example, when we stood in front of a huge post office building, wanting to mail our letters, we couldn't find a mailbox. At last, Paul asked a man passing by and he showed us the mailbox right in front of us. The situation had become so ridiculous, we felt so silly, that we started laughing uncontrollably. Humour really helped our situation.

Yonge Street downtown was an eye-opener. I had never seen such a crowded and busy street with such a variety of shops and displays, sometimes of unusual items. In the west end I saw women walking on the street with rollers in their hair. What a strange world!

Paul had a serious talk with the counsellor at Manpower about renting an apartment in the Queen and Lansdowne area, at 103 and 105 West Lodge Avenue. It was known as a slum area, though the two-building high-rise complex, built in a semi-circle with a water fountain in the middle that was lit up at night, was new. There were indoor garages, an indoor swimming pool and even air conditioning. Because Manpower paid our first month's rent, they were the ones who decided whether we could move in. Today I know how right they were in not wanting us to be in that area, but we weren't experienced enough to see the disadvantages. Paul used the fact that there was no lease to sign to convince the counsellor to give his approval. We moved to 103 West Lodge Avenue and the Acs moved into the next building. In the same building lived Lolla Horna and her two grown-up sons, Yurko and Janko. Mishko later became a very close friend of Janko, who was at least five years older.

We gradually found out that the counsellor had been right. The fire alarm went off almost every night and in the morning we would see a burned chesterfield thrown out onto the lawn. This was routine. The garage was full of broken glass bottles and often we were unable to sleep because of the noise from neighbours' parties; they seemed to be people who didn't work as we did and didn't have to get up early. Once, I tried to go to the source of noise on the upper floor to ask them to quiet down. The apartment door was slightly ajar and when I slowly opened it, I froze. The chairs placed in a semi-circle were empty and finished liquor bottles lay on the floor. Couples lay on divans, too busy with each other to detect a stranger in the room. Some seemed stoned to me. The radio was roaring. There was no one to talk to. Hopeless, I returned to our apartment.

Věra's father, Cornel, had a friend who was the owner of the Regal Constellation Hotel, close to the airport. He had promised her father that he would give Paul a job at the reception desk but when Paul went to see him, he said that he didn't have any opening at the reception desk and had only made the promise to Cornel in the hopes that Paul would more easily gain entrance to Canada. This was absolutely not necessary – Paul just needed a job. After Cornel's intervention, Paul got a job in the kitchen. What a disappointment – it was hard for him in every way. A hundred times a day he had to go in and out of the huge deep freezer, back and forth from the warm kitchen to the ice-cold freezer. There was a friendly German chef who liked Paul and tried to be a good colleague. They talked a lot during their lunch and coffee breaks and slowly this guy confided in Paul that at home he had been a friend of Göring and other Nazi officials. What a shock!

The next blow came on the following Sunday when Paul was reading the paper at home. Going through the employment advertisements, his eyes focused on an ad from the Regal Constellation, seeking a receptionist. What a jungle this world is! When Paul inquired about the job the next day, it was made clear to him that they had no intention of filling it with a newcomer. We soon found out that there is a quiet battle to be fought at all times, and that it is necessary to be aggressive to succeed.

I got a job on Queen Street in a paint factory and I tried to fit into the unfamiliar setting of blue-collar workers. As much as I wanted to keep the job that I desperately needed, I had to quit because I couldn't stand the paint fumes, which had been giving me headaches for a week.

We next found out about the Open Window Bakery, a business owned by four people of Hungarian and Czechoslovak origin. Paul called and talked to Max, the president. He asked how long Paul had been in Canada and wondered how good his English was. After a longer talk, Max told Paul to come and see him and to bring me along.

Max gave us both jobs. Paul got a job managing the plant and I got a job in shipping at the same place. It was at the far north end of the city. Paul had a car but because we worked different shifts, I had to take public transportation, which was long and complicated. One trip, in which I had to change from the subway and take another two buses, took me an hour and a half. Paul started work when I finished and we rarely saw each other, aside from half an hour in the afternoon before he started. This half-hour was precious time together. Once a week we had the same day off, which was very special to us.

At the bakery, one of the bosses greeted me in the morning with, "How are you?" but the next second he was gone. I couldn't find him to answer. When I spotted him in the next five minutes, I just wanted to tell him how I was, but he was busy. When I told Paul about the dilemma with the boss, he smiled and explained to me that on this continent, it was just a formality, just a greeting. At home, when we were asked how we were, we went into a lengthy explanation of our situation and the other person listened politely, taking part with interest in the conversation. Well, different country, different customs. It took time to find them out and get used to them.

For the first time in Michal's life, he liked his school and his teacher. The school, near Queen and Lansdowne, was in a very poor area and people were different, sincere and understanding. None of the children who emigrated in 1968 and came from schools in Czechoslovakia knew English but the Czechoslovak school curriculum was much more advanced, at least one grade ahead. The children back home also had stronger discipline in school. The language was no barrier for them – they quickly mastered English and, at the same time, progressed well enough to pass the course at the end of the year.

One evening I came home from work planning to take a pot of stuffed cabbage leaves in tomato sauce out from the fridge but couldn't find it. Then I saw the empty pot on the stove and Michal with a guilty expression on his face. He explained that he had praised my cooking to his pals and his teacher, none of whom had ever eaten this kind of food and were curious. So, Michal invited them over to taste it. They liked it so much that it had been finished to the last drop. I didn't mind that much. I was pleased that they liked my cooking and it just meant that I had to improvise a quick dinner.

Every day, we had to adjust to our new and different lifestyle. For example, Mirka, Steve's daughter, had been sent home from class one morning to change because she was wearing pants and a sweater, which was apparently not according to the rules. The teacher said that she had to wear a skirt over her pants. We had never before heard such a thing. Many such regulations were so strange to us. People were not allowed to drink alcoholic beverages on their own balconies or in their own gardens. In those days, there was an excellent program on TV that satirized such idiotic laws and regulations. We loved to watch it and the ratings were high.

Twice a week, in the evenings, I went with Steve to the neighbouring school to attend an English-as-a-Second-Language course. It was good to brush up on my English and it was also a relief for both of us to talk about our problems, getting out worries that we didn't want to burden our spouses with. Although the course finished at 10:00 p.m. and I had to get up for work at 5:00 a.m., it was still worthwhile for me to do it.

We had been in Canada for only two months when the pre-Christmas season approached. Again there were completely new experiences of this season for us, so different from Europe. Here, everything exceeds the old country. For example, Vienna – a Western, enterprising business city in the middle of Europe – has wonderfully decorated main streets at Christmastime, but here, the balconies of high-rise buildings and front of private houses, as well as trees on the streets, are lit with colourful Christmas bulbs. Our eyes had to get used to such an overwhelming spectacle. We considered it rather frivolous at first; within a few years, however, we changed our minds and started to like it.

We celebrated our first Christmas modestly in our apartment

with Lolla Horna and the Acs family. I used to celebrate Christmas with my aunt Anny and this was the first year that I had not made Christmas cookies. Our household was still not complete. The evening had a nostalgic tone. We were still terribly homesick but tried bravely not to admit it.

Paul soon got promoted to day-time manager, overseeing the chain of stores in the city. Both the bosses and the employees discovered that he was smart and knowledgeable and started to respect and like him. He cared about employees' rights and stood up for them.

A couple of months later, I got an offer to work at Cake Master, one of the most prestigious confectionery and delicatessen stores in the city, near the Colonnade at Avenue Road and Bloor Street. I took the job because we were thinking of possibly buying a store of our own in the future and thought that working there would give me an opportunity to look deeper into the profession, learn some good tricks and get a feeling for this kind of business. The owners were Georgina, originally from Budapest, and her husband, Paul Rigor, from Žilina, Slovakia, a friend of my mother-in-law's brother Bela Bací.

The Rigors had left Slovakia in the 1950s and lived in Paris for a couple of years. After they came to Canada, they started a small bakery on Bathurst Street and worked very hard. They then convinced one of the best confectioners, a man named Fred, who had worked in a famous Viennese hotel, to work for them. It was a wise move. They moved to the store in Yorkville, on Cumberland Street, where they became the most famous, though expensive, store with European specialties. They did well and their customers were well established, many of them from the Hungarian and Czechoslovak elite, mixed with artists and writers, including the well-known Hungarian writer George Jonas. In the corner of the store was a huge oval table, always occupied with steady customers. They were served salads, pâtés, sandwiches, coffee, tea and pastries.

There were three salesladies, including me. In the morning I had to take the fresh pastries out of the oven and arrange them on trays for the window and store display. Later I was either behind the counter or serving the tables. During the time that I was arranging pastries in the back of the store, I listened to Paul and Fred's discussions in German about the daily stock market, investments, antique sales and auctions, which was quite interesting and gave me an idea how well off these people really were.

The Rigors were an intelligent and sophisticated couple. My first two days in the store, Georgina taught me the secrets of how to take care of pastries, the selling and the overall tricks of the profession. I remember her telling me to be her shadow and learn all I needed to know. I enjoyed sales and talking to people. In a way, it was a challenge for me. Unfortunately, things soon started to change. Georgina kept an eye on me and criticized me often, and the atmosphere grew oppressive. A Czech customer, knowing how recently I had come to Canada, approached me with a question about how things were in Czechoslovakia. Georgina stopped me from answering, saying that the store was my work place and not a coffee house. As I led the Czech couple to a table, I noticed their embarrassment.

After work one evening as I entered the corridor on our floor, I started to hear the beautiful melody of George Gershwin's "Night and Day" near our apartment. I stopped for a few seconds, listening, enjoying the wonderful moment, the stress of the day dissolving. Coming closer to our door, the music got louder. As I stood for a while in front of the door, I started to realize that the music was coming from our apartment. I opened the door and saw Paul grinning at me. I was looking at a huge Telefunken music system. I looked at Paul with questioning eyes. We certainly did not have the money to afford such a luxury. In answer, Paul said, "I realized how badly we need to recover at home with music." He was right.

～

Paul had a good sense for business and got deeply involved in his work at the bakery. The idea that we would buy our own bakery or delicatessen store slowly faded. We discussed the possibility many times and were aware how difficult it would be for us to succeed in this business, considering the long hours and other obstacles. A large family could take shifts, but we would have to hire help and still one of us would have to be in the store to have control over everything. We considered it to be too high a price for an inexperienced family, with the risk of losing money and having no family life.

We also finally decided that life at West Lodge Avenue was not for us. We were earning more money and began looking for a nicer apartment in a better area. We liked an apartment on Thorncliffe Park Drive very much, an elegant complex of high-rise buildings with a recreation centre and an indoor and outdoor pool.

Thorncliffe Park Drive was shaped in a large circle, with a plaza full of shops in the middle and surrounded by buildings. Its green lawns, shrubs, trees and creatively planted, colourful flowers reminded me of a spa rather than a street, with public tennis courts and quiet rest places with benches.

We were hesitant because of the higher rent. However, in the end we decided on a two-bedroom apartment on the third floor with a wonderful view of the surrounding park. The apartment was full of daylight and sun, which lifted my spirits. The Schanzers helped us move. When we followed the huge moving truck with all our modest belongings along the Lakeshore in our Saab, knowing that we would be living in a better place, I got very emotional but tried to hide it.

Slowly, our future seemed to be more promising. We soon discovered that there was a small community of Slovak and Czech people around us. One lady whom we got to know, Lily Novak, was from Prague and had two boys Michal's age. Lolla and the Acs also moved into the area. We started to meet new families and arrange visits and walks together as did our children, who found friends. We continued to meet more people of Slovak origin living in our community. Zoli and Anna Green soon invited us over with a group of people. Zoli had been a pediatrician back home, but in Canada he had to prepare for new exams. I became friends with Anna, whom everyone called Nushi. They had a son, Yurko, and an older daughter, Jana. There were also the Werners and Dr. Kraus, an orthopedic surgeon, and Eda, a quiet man, his wife, Gabi, who was full of energy, and their two daughters. As soon as Gabi laid eyes on me, she said she knew me, but at the moment could not place me right away. Ten minutes later she got kind of excited, saying that I had been in Auschwitz, in the medical block, sick with typhus, lying on the third bunk. Everyone stopped talking, amazed by such a coincidence. I was so ill at that time that I didn't remember her. We started to talk about these times and everything she said fit into place. Everyone was fascinated by this turn of events, which left us all bringing back deep memories of hard times.

Establishing Ourselves

In 1970, I started playing with the idea of retraining for an office job. Paul encouraged me to apply for a course at Manpower to upgrade my high school education. I had to quit my job to qualify and the waiting period was very difficult. I got restless and phoned Manpower every week until the counsellor finally got upset, telling me to be patient until I heard from them. Finally, I got a letter advising me of the starting date for my course. After graduating, I would be allowed to take a full-time commercial course. The classes at George Brown College took place at different campuses across the city and I went to almost all of them. I was happy, eager to start, excited and also a little afraid.

A lot of young dropouts were in the class. It would have been no problem to buy marijuana in any class, if you were interested, but I didn't go for that. I smoked cigarettes but was afraid to start using marijuana or any other drugs. The teachers were great and I learned so much from them. The class was an international mix of students born in Toronto and those coming from Asia, Europe and all over the world. My favourite subject was literature because we had great discussions. We also learned about Canada's system of government, which was new to me. The subject I liked least was mathematics. I mastered the basics and I was top in my class, but I had forgotten fractions. If Paul and Michal had not spent numerous hours with me, patiently explaining the material, I wouldn't have made it through the course.

After the high school course, I continued on to the commercial course. The typewriter keyboard in English is a little different from the Czech so I had to forget my previous training and start as every beginner does, blindfolded, to master the keyboard. I never could satisfy my typing teacher. She always said, "You can do better." I thought that she was picking on me, but how right she was! Without her support I never could have achieved the excellent result of sixty-five strokes per minute by graduation time.

In October 1971 it was almost time to graduate from the course. I had spent one and a half years doing these courses and felt able to face the business world. I was eager to find a job and actively started looking by signing up with a job agency and taking various tests. A counsellor interviewed me about my work expectations and I completed numerous applications. They sent me to many companies, where again I completed tests and applications, but no one hired me. My typing was excellent and my spelling was very, very good, so I thought it must be my accent. I also would have accepted an accounting job, which was one of the subjects I had completed. However, I always got a friendly answer that they would contact me, which never happened. At one time I was told that I had no Canadian experience. I was already so upset that my answer was, "Certainly, if you don't give me a chance, I will never get it." I had graduated with honours. I was in touch with some of the students from my class and heard that since Christmas was coming, there was no point in going out to look for a job. Also, if I didn't find a job, there was always a possibility of collecting unemployment cheques.

My counsellor called me one day to let me know that she thought she had found the right job for me. She told me to go to the Canadian Red Cross Society on Wellesley Street East. The old routine of tests was repeated endlessly. At the end, the personnel officer gave me a long questionnaire to complete. Being already so tired and discouraged, I asked her why I should complete it. She said, "Because you're hired." I couldn't believe it! My background and knowledge of lan-

guages were valuable assets for my future work at Red Cross headquarters, in the tracing and reunion of families department. I had to
pinch myself to believe that it was not a dream. I went home so happy.
It was such a lift for me, after so many disappointments, to have succeeded in one of my goals. I went to buy a new outfit, as I wanted
to look good, and bought a stunning black-and-white pantsuit. Paul
said I looked wonderful in it.

Early the following Monday I stood in front of an old building of
neo-gothic style. The previous owners of this building were a well-off
Toronto family and I later found out that in 1938 the assessed value
of $8,500,000 had been offset by a sizable donation made to the Red
Cross by the widow, Mrs. Sarah Warren. The interior originally consisted of a ballroom, which became the boardroom, the music room,
which became the national executive office, and the dining room,
which was now the library. Other rooms on the ground floor and
upper floors had been turned into administrative and service offices. A massive wooden staircase of Spanish handiwork led up to
the newer family bedroom suites, each with fireplaces and baths. The
original servants' quarters on the third floor were later rebuilt into
small offices.

At the switchboard was Miss Johnson, a handsome, tall, friendly
woman. Everyone called her "Johny." She looked at me with great authority and, hearing that I was starting my new job, she proclaimed,
"My dear, women at the Red Cross do not wear pants. It is our policy." I was surprised, but I couldn't have changed anyway. I gave her a
smile and went up the staircase. By my third day, though, the funniest
thing happened – Johny came to the office wearing pants. The policy
was broken.

When I stepped into the office of Colonel Price, director of international affairs, he looked at me, whistled and gave me a big smile.
He welcomed me warmly. Mr. Price went with me to the next office
to introduce me to my immediate boss, Mrs. Simpson. The office, in
one of the previous bedrooms, had a fireplace and a bay window with

a gorgeous view of east and west Wellesley Street, and my desk was right in front of the window. I couldn't have asked for a better seat.

Mrs. Simpson was a slim, tiny woman in her mid-sixties with white hair, an attractive face and sweet smile. She explained to me the kind of work I would be doing. We were tracing missing persons through certain channels and all information was confidential. We were also involved in tracing people in disaster situations and the network of sister organizations was international. The work sounded extremely interesting.

Our kitchen was on the ground floor – a large, old-style beauty with a huge tile oven. In the middle of the kitchen was an oval table with twelve matching chairs that was considered the support staff's cafeteria. There was a lot going on and people were friendly. The executives went to restaurants and snack bars, which were plentiful in the neighbourhood. These "bosses" acted as a hierarchy – there was an unwritten policy of not mingling with support staff. Once, a colleague of mine expressed, truthfully, "They are impressed by their own importance." There were only two exceptions, Colonel Price and, later, his successor, George Weber, who came from the Swiss Red Cross office in Geneva. George was always down-to-earth, smart and ambitious. He was the youngest-ever executive of such a high rank. In later years he was named commissioner of the Canadian Red Cross and around 1992 became secretary-general of the International Federation of the Red Cross and Red Crescent Societies in Geneva.

George Weber always talked to me as a friend and used to bring us little presents from his trips. When we had a heavy work week, on Fridays he brought us each a rose. I made close friends at the national office. I remember that my first day there, when I went to the kitchen, a friendly blond woman greeted me by saying, "Don't feel lonely, my dear. Come and visit us in the library any time." Her name was Jos and she was originally from Holland. Her husband, Stanley, was from Poland and they had come to Canada in the 1950s. There was another lady in the library, Anna, of Hungarian origin. She was well educated and intelligent and spoke five languages fluently. She and Jos were the official translators at the Red Cross. Then there was Theresa, a dear woman originally from Greece. She was the secretary to the secretary of the Red Cross. We all started to see each other outside work, along with Stanley and Paul, and became close friends. Unfortunately, quite a few years later, Theresa developed Alzheimer's disease and started slowly deteriorating. It was heartbreaking to see her at the end; she couldn't recognize any of us. She died in a nursing home.

I soon felt as though my immediate boss, Mrs. Simpson, was acting unkind to me. She was an Anglo-Saxon Canadian and it felt to me as though she didn't like Jews and immigrants. What an irony, working at the Red Cross! Her grudge against me really started when she found out that I was a good worker, that I spoke a few languages and might be serious competition. Mr. Price wanted me to take over after she retired, which was already due. She was petty and my daily life with her began to be difficult.

Mr. Price was a cheerful man; he made his rounds every day through the office, humming opera arias or joking. One Friday afternoon Mr. Price left the office early to play golf. We later heard that soon after he started playing, he suffered a heart attack and died immediately. For a long time we couldn't get him out of our minds. Many people mourned him; he was such a cheerful man, a good human being.

Mr. Rush, the administrative manager, was named to act on his behalf until a suitable individual could be named for the post of director for international affairs. My work situation deteriorated, as he was close to Mrs. Simpson. If I didn't pay too much attention to her petty requests, she went to Mr. Rush, complaining. I was upset and felt close to a nervous breakdown. I quietly did my work and tried not to react to Mrs. Simpson's silly remarks. However, when Mr. Rush came into our office every afternoon, he would go up to Mrs. Simpson with a coffee cup in his hands and ask her, "Would you, Mrs. Simpson, do me the honour of pouring me a coffee?" It drove me up the wall.

After almost six years at the national office, an opportunity came for me to transfer to the Toronto branch in the next building. There was an opening there for a tracing officer with the tracing and reunion department and I applied for the job. I made an appointment with Ron McClory, the executive director of the Toronto branch. We talked about my previous work in Prague and Ron was impressed hearing that I had worked for IBM. I got the job easily.

My life changed completely. I was myself again. I got promoted to coordinator of tracing and reunion of families. People in that department were different – kind, helpful, sincere. The atmosphere was pleasant. The Ontario division, to which we reported, was on the third floor. I made many new friends and am still in touch with some of them. I was very close to Lucille, from Trinidad, and Fernando, from Cuba, who worked in accounting. Sometimes the three of us went to the Red Lion pub across from our office after work for a chat and a drink. Two years later, there was a sudden change in Fernando's appearance. He didn't feel well and he once showed us his leg, which had turned partly black. We then knew that it was bad. We were shocked when he lost a lot of weight and had other complications. Soon, he couldn't work anymore. It turned out that he had full-blown AIDS and was dying. That was around 1977, a few years before the epidemic officially began. I was asked to initiate a request with the Red Cross in Cuba and the Cuban government for permission for his mother to visit him in Canada. The request was denied and a couple of months later, Fernando died. I saw other people dying of this terrible disease and I never got used to it.

I reported to Millie, director of international services at the Ontario division, and we later became friends. Originally from Jamaica, she was intelligent and a good diplomat; it was a pleasure to work with her and I got to know her whole family. My immediate boss, Helen Kiely – who right away told everyone, "Call me Babs" – was a very special person. She was a nurse by profession and helpful wherever she could be. A small, round woman on short legs, she walked exactly like a duck. She was funny, sincere and a perfectionist. Everything in her home had to be in order. Her soup packages had to be lined up alphabetically. Anywhere she went, either to a hotel or a hospital, she straightened out the chairs when they were not exactly to her liking, lining them up like soldiers.

It was a blow for me when she came to the office one day and said that she had been diagnosed with breast cancer; the illness was progressing quite quickly. What an irony. A nurse, who her whole life took care of everyone around her, was now struck with a dreadful, fatal illness. She was unable to work for long at the office and got weaker and weaker. Luckily, she lived close to the office. I was able to visit her almost every day during my lunch break and brought her my cooking in little pots, fed her and brushed her hair. It was so sad knowing that I would not be able to do it much longer. They took her to the hospital after she had almost died in my arms. Her daughter called me a few hours after I left the hospital to say that she had passed away. How many times would I have to go through the intense sadness of losing a friend?

My work was my salvation. I looked forward to coming to the office every day. When I went to bed every night I thought about what I could improve, what other goals I could achieve. I loved my work and realized how lucky I was to be doing it. I was searching for missing persons for families who had lost contact with each other under a variety of circumstances. At times, we made an exception and accepted a request for friends. For me, it was like putting together a puzzle. I interviewed clients to obtain information and forwarded this information to sister societies in other countries around the world. It was necessary to obtain as much information as possible to make the search relatively feasible.

The scope of our department was vast. We were involved in disasters that occurred anywhere – here in Canada or in other countries around the globe – and finding out if relatives were alive, injured or evacuated. We dealt with refugees, with regard to their social welfare, and we dealt with the government, embassies or any office that advocates on behalf of individuals who needed our assistance. My knowledge of languages was a real asset. I learned to deal with people and after years of practice I was good at it. My background helped me deal with anyone as a human being, no matter what race, religion or nationality. I was proud to follow the principles of the Red Cross, to be impartial and neutral. There were many times that I fought on behalf of some families to continue with a case when it had been closed. How fortunate I was to have had an opportunity to be involved in such humanitarian work.

The Red Cross is based on volunteer work and throughout my time there, I worked with many volunteers who became my friends. One day the director of volunteers introduced me to a tall, gray-haired woman with an elegant posture whose name was Grace. Before retiring, she had been a secretary to the president of a large corporation. Grace had wonderful skills we could use and we worked well together – there was an amazing chemistry between us. Throughout the years I learned a lot from her with regard to composing letters and expressing myself clearly and efficiently in the rich English language.

Grace and I became very fond of each other and built up a wonderful friendship. If we don't meet, we at least speak to each other every evening on the phone. I have to say that she is one of the kindest people I have ever met. She is intelligent and well read. We enjoy discussing matters on any subject. We respect each other and I feel privileged to be her friend.

John was another volunteer who had retired early. He was stunningly handsome and impeccably, expensively dressed. He wore a bowtie and looked like a real gentleman, as he indeed was. John's strength was phone inquiries, searching for people or interviewing people. He had been living with his partner, Bob, for twenty years. Bob was a librarian and they lived in a condominium downtown. John was such a caring person and he worried about Bob, who had a heart condition. When Bob died of heart failure, John was devastated. He grieved and stuck by us, taking strength from our friendship. Bob's family took John under their wing and fully accepted him as a member of their family.

~

During my first year at the Red Cross, I reunited with my father's cousin Karl, who lived in Canada. I had been fairly sure that he lived in Montreal and, when I found his telephone number, I called him. I had always thought that he was a man who cared about family and indeed he was thrilled to hear from me. He and my father had been close. We talked for a long time and agreed that he would visit us with his wife, Emmy.

Karl must have been in his middle sixties – he had a soft face without wrinkles, white, fly-away hair, and had the look of a typical artist. He was a professor at McGill University in Montreal, and also held concerts and taught music. Karl was so pleased to see me and my family. His wife, Emmy, was a striking redhead with a fine complexion who was more than twenty years younger than him, smart and full of energy. They stayed with us for two days and we caught up on old times, reminiscing about everyone in the family who was not with us anymore. He recalled a lot that I was glad to find out.

I remembered Karl from when I was six years old and our large family met in Brno at my grandparents' fiftieth wedding anniversary. Karl was living in Vienna with his wife, Lisa, at the time. He was a music professor and a student of Austrian composer and teacher Arnold Schönberg. Karl admired Schönberg and strictly followed his experimental teachings in atonality, although he also continued working with traditional classical music. I was unable to see any beauty in Schönberg's kind of atonal music. Although I was musically trained and grew up in a musical home, I could never remember one sound of a melody.

After Austria was annexed by Germany in 1938, Karl and Lisa, like many Viennese Jews, were sent to the Dachau concentration camp.

However, the "famous" and rich lawyer of the family, Uncle Josef, was able to use his influential connections to arrange Karl's and Lisa's discharge from Dachau. This rarely happened, but at that time it worked. Karl and Lisa took refuge in Shanghai, China, where he earned his living by playing pop music in bars. After the war, they immigrated to Canada. They eventually divorced, but maintained a good friendship. Karl later met and married Emmy.

Karl and Emmy visited us a few times. They appreciated my good cooking and I was glad that they enjoyed their time with us. Their older son, Nicholas, is an opera singer and music teacher. The younger, Bruno, is a health therapist by profession, but as a hobby he plays in a rock orchestra. I don't know if Karl disapproved, but he was a good father and didn't pressure them to follow his opinions.

Some time after this visit, Paul travelled to Vienna. His parents had owned a large apartment building there and since his father had passed away in 1962, Mother, Peter and Paul had finally decided to sell it. While Paul was away and I was alone with Mishko for three weeks, he developed a bad cold with high fever and had to stay home. Although he was still sick, he had an important test at school and I agreed that he could go as long as he came home right after. When he hadn't arrived home by 5:00 p.m., I was nervous. I called the school, but there was no answer. I called friends to check if by any chance he was there, but he was nowhere to be found. Eventually, I contacted the police to report him missing. I was out of my mind with worry. The police officer came to the apartment, asking for every detail.

When there was finally a knock on the door, there was Mishko, seemingly okay, with an uncertain smile and an embarrassed look. How glad I was to see him! It turned out that there had been an important basketball match to play in Hamilton after the test. He was one of the best players and his friends had persuaded him that he had to be there. He apparently had no time to telephone, as they had boarded the buses right away. I think that I convinced him that this was the first and the last time anything like that could happen. I called the police to report that the missing kid was alive and well. I was very glad when Paul returned from Europe.

Around this same time, Paul felt that we should start looking for a house to buy. I wasn't so certain, but Paul was adamant. So, in 1971, we went house hunting. It was interesting to see different kinds of houses and households, seeing how people lived. It was also exhausting, but we were in no hurry and took our time. Then, Paul came home one day announcing that he had seen a house he liked, a bungalow with a huge garden on a quiet street near Finch and Bayview. That was quite far north of the city then and, to me, at the end of the world. The city was building a subway station at Finch, but it wouldn't be running for about a year. I was reluctant to see the house but Paul said he really wanted me to see it.

I liked it right away. The house was a wood-panelled bungalow with a heavy wooden front door. Immediately inside was a small hall, then, a few steps away, a large living room with a beautiful view into a well-kept garden and patio. The house had three bedrooms and the kitchen was a beauty. A huge Chinese cherry tree in bloom decorated the view into the garden. From a side door, steps led to a finished basement with two large rooms, a laundry room, a pantry and a door to the garage. The garden had three rows of long flower beds that were professionally planted so that from April to September one flower replaced the other. The price was right and there was no reason not to buy it, so we did. At the beginning it was a real adventure to stroll through the house and discover new corners and new cupboards. The previous owners had left us a ping-pong table and other sporting goods that we appreciated. For the first time, we were house owners. It was the beginning of a new era and it was exciting.

Some time ago, Miško had asked to have a dog and we always told him that there wasn't enough space in an apartment. Now was the time to stick to our promise. We first consulted a friend who was a veterinarian about the kind of dog to choose and then Paul got an offer from one of the bakers who had a farm close to Toronto. He had a few mixed Labrador puppies and invited Paul and Mishko to come the following Sunday. When I heard the car coming into our driveway that Sunday, I ran through the kitchen and there, under the staircase, was a black puppy with huge brown eyes looking at me. How adorable and sweet he was! He was happy and appreciative of our attention, but we found out that there were moments, especially when we made sudden movements like putting on coats or opening a newspaper, that he ran from us as if he were being hunted. There was something wrong and we came to think that he must have been abused at the farm. We had to show him a lot of love to gain his trust. We decided that Mishko should name him and he chose Ami, which means friend in French. After about a year, we noticed such a change in him – he turned into a happy, trusting, healthy dog.

After we moved into the house, Mother came to visit us for a few months – it was her second visit. She had gotten on in years and didn't understand the lifestyle and customs of this continent, but hadn't we all wondered at the beginning? She had a few friends here her age, but mostly she stayed home by herself the whole day. She didn't understand English, which was difficult. Paul got some Hungarian books from the library for her and she could call her friends on the phone, but we worked during the day and she understandably looked forward to us coming home. In the evenings we translated TV programs for her, but honestly, it was very tiring. We took her out on weekends and tried to show her Toronto, Niagara Falls, all the interesting places. We also took her to a Jewish wedding, the kind of lavish event that we had never known at home, hoping that she would enjoy these new experiences.

Milestones

When we moved to the north end of the city, Mišhko didn't change schools. Although he didn't have close friends at Leaside High School and there were good schools much closer, he just decided to finish high school there. He never complained, but years later we found out that he and his immigrant pals had had a hard time there. We remembered that on his first day at school he told us that children asked them what their fathers did. If the answer was not a profession such as a lawyer or doctor, they turned away, dismissing their existence. I also heard that there was an "immigrants' table" in the cafeteria that was completely ignored. Leaside was in a predominantly Anglo-Saxon area. There were apparently other acts of discrimination and I'm afraid that this era left Mišhko with a bad feeling about Canada. We weren't aware of the extent of the problem at the time. We went to parents' meetings but Mišhko's grades dropped. Although we discussed this with him, I think that he lost confidence in us. He may have even been trying to protect us from one more problem. With more experience, I might have handled the situation better.

The end result was that Mišhko came home one day and told us that he would probably travel the world after finishing high school. We didn't take him seriously at first, but after a while we saw that he meant it. What could we have done? We asked him to reconsider but it was no use. We told him that we would support his studies at a university in Toronto, but we wouldn't give him any money for his travels. He accepted this and made some money by working with the Canada Bread company. He soon bought a plane ticket with a friend and went to England, promising to stay in touch.

Three weeks later we received a letter saying that he and his friend had parted ways and Mišhko had gone to Bordeaux, France. He had gotten a job in the vineyards and was learning to speak French because the owners didn't speak English. Then, we didn't hear from him for six weeks. This was a terrible time for us. Sitting silently in the evenings, we were unable to console each other. A dark cloud of helplessness hung over our heads. Finally, we got a letter from Rome. In Mišhko's great literary style he described his journey, the cities he had stopped in and his adventures. It seemed that he was thinking a lot, realizing that he was experiencing real life, relying only on himself. He accepted any kind of work he could get.

I found out later that there were days he didn't have any work or any food to eat. I'm glad that I didn't know about it at the time. He decided to go to Israel next and soon wrote us from the south. He was in Eilat, staying on the beach in a sleeping bag. While he was there he met Hana, a student at the Hebrew University of Jerusalem who was working in a kiosk selling food and drinks for the summer, and they fell deeply in love. Hana was taking courses in pedagogy and a special course in dance and music as a therapeutic method for disabled children. Her parents, of Polish origin, lived in Jerusalem, where they had immigrated when their two children were still babies. Hana's father was a geologist and took a post in the diplomatic corps in South America, where Hana learned Spanish. She later lived in France for two years and spoke French, as well as Polish, English and Hebrew.

Mišhko wanted to study archaeology but later decided on history. As I mentioned before, we were not willing to pay for his studies outside of Canada, hoping that he would return. But we were wrong. He found work in a few kibbutzim (community farms) where he became familiar with the Hebrew language. He then decided to take an intensive Hebrew course that was offered free. This time and circumstances affected his future. His eventual return to Canada was only for the sake of making good money for his studies in Israel. Paul arranged a hard but well-paying job in the bakery. Mishko then returned to Israel and enrolled at Tel Aviv University, taking general history and English literature.

In 1979, Mishko and Hana came to Toronto, where they got married. They stayed in our house briefly and then returned to Israel. I have not seen a couple so much in love and we were glad. Hana was an intelligent woman with a wonderful personality.

Paul and I had a busy social life in Toronto. We had lots of friends and Paul's colleagues often invited him to weddings and bar or bat mitzvahs. Paul worked long hours, six days a week, and badly needed Sunday to relax, so I didn't pressure him to do housework. He got the shopping done and took care of financial and other matters. We had a gardener, but I always lent a hand to keep the garden neat and clean. Although we also had a cleaning woman, I still did a lot of heavy work around the house. It was getting to be too much for me. I wanted to move into a condominium with excellent transportation options that was walking distance to a shopping plaza and had a recreation centre right in the building.

It was not easy to convince Paul. He was comfortable where we were and I didn't want to nag him. After two years of thinking about it, he realized that my wish for an easier life was legitimate. Typical for Paul, as soon as he made up his mind, he got enthusiastic about the plan. We started looking at apartments and saw one in our area that we really fell in love with. On the thirty-second floor, it was 1,700-square feet, laid out in a semi-circle, and looked out north, west and east with a spectacular view in the evening of flickering lights on the highways and roads. Watching life from such a perspective gave me a sense of tranquility and peace. There was a wonderful well-kept recreation centre in the basement, indoor and outdoor swimming pools, tennis courts, a sauna, a squash court, ping-pong and billiards, a card room, a library and a lounge.

Paul went to work the next morning and before lunch he surprised me by phoning to say that he had bought the apartment. Again, this was typical of Paul. I was glad, but I also knew things were going to be complicated for a while. We had to put our house up for sale and Paul speculated that if it did not sell soon, we would have to get a bridge loan. I tried to be optimistic, but Paul got worried and couldn't sleep. Soon, seeing him in such a nervous state, I joined him in sleepless nights. People who were interested in buying the house made appointments they didn't keep. A few times, coming home from work, people were already waiting for us in the driveway. We had dinners at the strangest times and the house always had to be in perfect order. Finally, a large young man, a popular American football player, liked the house and bought it on the spot. It was such a relief.

We moved on December 30, 1980, and took great pleasure in decorating our new home. We bought some new furniture and consulted each other before hanging up a painting; we analyzed and debated every little change we made. When we were ready, we invited our friends for housewarming parties. We had four parties, each with about twenty-five people.

Within a year, the Greens moved into the building because as soon as they saw our apartment and the recreation centre, they loved it. Paul and I began going to art auctions. It was fascinating to learn more about paintings, sculptures and Persian rugs. Paul borrowed library books about art so that when we went to the auctions, we were able to use our knowledge in assessing the items. Sometimes we were lucky enough to buy a good piece of art for a reasonable price. On our way home, we would discuss on which wall we would put the new painting or which spot would best suit our new carpet. It was a stimulating and thrilling feeling to be able, for the second time in our life, to furnish a new home with art according to our taste.

In the summer of 1982, we visited Hana and Miško in Israel.

They lived in Herzliya, one of the nicest suburbs of Tel Aviv, close to the ocean, to embassies and to modern hotels. They were both still studying at the university, which was fairly close to their home. It was a little rented house with a small garden full of cactuses and tropical plants, decorated with ancient oil containers and other old and beautiful objects.

While we were in Israel, we also spent time with my brother-in-law, Rolland Černy, who always made a special effort to take us to many interesting places in the country. He was by then seventy-two years old and, although he passed away the following year, was still a doctor practising at a few hospitals throughout the country. We travelled by car through Druze villages and, although people told us that it wouldn't be safe for us to be there with an Israeli license plate because people would throw stones at us, that never happened. On the contrary, when we stepped out of the car at a bazaar to buy some little presents, people were friendly. Then we visited Lake Kinneret near Tiberias.

While I was on my own there, I strolled through the market, which was absolutely packed with Arabs, Druzes and nomads with camels or donkeys. It was a real mixture of the Middle East, very noisy, with women whose faces were covered with black cloth so that just their eyes were showing. All of a sudden I felt uneasy, worrying about what would happen if someone objected to seeing a woman dressed in Western clothes on her own. I didn't understand any Arabic. I panicked and went to the bank to find Paul, but I didn't see him. Then I got really scared. The five minutes that Paul was gone seemed to me like hours. I screamed at him hysterically that he should not have left me in this strange world. I did calm down after a while, but I will never forget this moment of fear. Later, on the road from Nazareth to Tiberias, Rolland took us to an Arab restaurant called Younes, which he said served excellent food. We ate the best fish I have ever tasted there.

We stopped at Kfar Nahum, said to be the home of Jesus, and

continued to Afula, Haifa and Nazareth. We explored the slopes of Mount Carmel, the residential area, where a new, modern university was built on the top. From there we could look down at the industrial part next to the extensive port and harbour facilities in the nearby Kishon River. Paul's cousin Stella lived on Mount Carmel with her husband, Bedřich, and family. We knew each other from Banská Bystrica. They had married at the same time as Paul and I, and shortly after left for Israel. We stayed with them for two days and our children surprised us by showing up the evening we arrived.

The next day, Stella and Bedřich drove us northeast along the foothills of the Galilee, passing Arab and Druze villages. We stopped further north at Kibbutz Hanita, where Mišhko had worked. The people in the kibbutz were friendly, especially when we mentioned that our son had worked with them. They gave us a tour and served us a wonderful lunch; we appreciated their hospitality. Then we continued south to Akko, a walled city on a small peninsula where a natural port had been created and used by Phoenicians and Romans, then greatly enlarged by Crusaders and restored by Turks. Continuing south, we reached Caesarea. We looked forward to visiting the famous Roman theatre dating from the first century B C E and Caesarea was also an important centre under the Crusaders. It is an unusual feeling visiting such ancient places, thinking about the history we have learned and the people who centuries ago had stepped on the same soil that we walked on. I had to take home at least a stone from every place to remind me, along with other mementos, of such precious legacies.

We also visited our close friends Luci and Vilko Schönfeld in Tel Aviv. The city is relatively modern; it was built in 1909 and rapidly developed under the British mandate, when Arab riots led many Jews to move to Tel Aviv from nearby Jaffa. On the eve of independence, after intense fighting, most of Jaffa's Arab population fled and, in 1950, the two cities united under the name Tel Aviv-Yafo (Jaffa). The main street is Dizengoff, named after the city's first mayor. The city has a completely different atmosphere from Jerusalem because it is newer and people are usually fashionably dressed in European-style clothing. There are many garden coffee houses, always full. Despite the frequent threat of terrorist attacks, people in Tel Aviv seem to live from one day to the next, taking from life all they can.

The most memorable trip we took with the Schönfelds was a visit to the ancient fortification of Masada overlooking the Dead Sea. A cable car took us to the top of the cliff, once the winter palace of Herod the Great and the last stronghold of Jewish zealots who fought against Roman conquest. The cable car doesn't travel down, so one has to walk down a path holding onto a railing; it was terrifying. At the foot, one overlooks the Dead Sea and nothing else except the sky.

After we had only been in Israel for a few days, the radio announced one morning that Israeli troops had invaded Lebanon. When we travelled by bus, all the drivers were listening to their small radios and informing passengers about the news on the front line, quietly following the army's progress. In this small country, almost everyone has a son, daughter or a relative in the army. Israel is a nation that was and is always called upon to defend its land and so almost everyone is familiar with the pain of losing a loved one.

We headed home, leaving the children promising to come soon to Canada, where life is so much easier and peaceful. We were glad when Hana and Miško came to Toronto shortly after our visit. Miško got a job at the Open Window Bakery and signed up for a correspondence course at the University of Toronto to continue his studies in history and English. Hana became familiar with the city within a week and got a job teaching Hebrew to adults in the evenings. To save money, they lived in our apartment and we all got along very well. After all, the apartment was large enough for everyone to be comfortable and have some privacy.

We really enjoyed this time of family companionship, but, after around one and a half years of living with us, the children decided to rent a house downtown. Hana found a house on Manning Street, in the Dundas-Bathurst area, and then found a job as a kindergarten teacher.

On July 12, 1984, a beautiful Sunday summer morning, Paul and I were invited to a swimming pool party at the house of our friends Anička and George. We chatted with friends and then sat down at a small table to have a delicious cold lunch prepared by the hostess, Anička. A tall, handsome man came to our table and noticed the number tattooed on my arm. He asked me if I had been in a concentration camp, as his wife had during World War II. Shortly after, his wife joined us. She was very pretty and friendly. We talked to each other about which camp we had been in and found we both had been in Theresienstadt at the same time, in the workplace. When I said that there had only been three girls in this workplace – Kathy, Hana and me – the woman answered, "Yes, I am Hana. Who are you?" I answered quietly and quite emotionally, "I am Gerti." Hana immediately cried out, "Oh, our little sister!" We embraced, weeping, as were the crowd around us.

Hana and Kathy were seventeen at the time and I was thirteen. We had soon thought of each other not only as friends but as sisters. I was tall, quite skinny and hungry most of the time; they tried to mother me as much as they could. After a few months, we were separated and transported to the East. After the war I often thought about Hana and Kathy, wondering if they were alive.

One day, when I met a friend on the street in Prague and we talked about the war, she mentioned Hana's name. I got excited when I heard that Hana had returned safely to Prague with her mother. My friend had given me their address in Karlín, a suburb of Prague and, soon after, I visited Hana and her mother. We were so happy to see each other again. We talked about Kathy, but had no idea whether she was still alive. Hana told me then that she was planning to move to England. She had met a handsome man of Czech origin who was a pilot of the British Royal Air Force and they planned to get married. Unfortunately, I lost contact with her. We were so unsure of our future and of ourselves that we sometimes couldn't think clearly. And now here we were, reunited by coincidence after thirty-seven years in a country far from Europe. This time, we kept in touch. Her husband, John, was intelligent, well read and kind, and we gladly included them in our circle of friends. As we get older and wiser, we know how to treasure such bonds of friendship and not lose it.

~

In the winter, we always went south for at least one week. In February 1985, my daughter-in-law, Hana, was pregnant, so we planned our vacation around being back in Toronto for the birth. Hana got so big that I once suggested to her that she might be having twins, but she dismissed the idea. According to her, the doctor had not mentioned this possibility. We decided to spend our one-week holiday in the Dominican Republic at a resort named Villa El Dorada, close to Puerto Plata on the Atlantic side.

I love stepping out of an airplane into warm weather; it takes away all my stress, lets me exhale my fatigue. The resort was located in a valley with Mount Isabel de Torres on one side and the ocean on the other. The green lawns with creatively decorated flower beds, tropical palms and blooming native trees were so soothing.

We relaxed in the garden, conversed with friendly vacationers and made small trips along the sugar plantations to the town and beaches of Sosúa, where a group of Jewish refugees were allowed to settle during World War II. We visited a woman in her nineties from the small Jewish community, who told us that most of the Jewish families had left for New York or other large US cities after the war because some Nazi families had moved into the town. Unfortunately, we couldn't visit the city's synagogue; it was closed because they were expecting a new, young rabbi from Israel. After we left the woman's home, Paul told me that, coincidentally, he and Luci Schönfeld had been among a group of children that might have been sent to Sosúa by a Jewish organization at the beginning of the war, but for some reason, the plan fell through.

We also visited the old colonial town of Puerto Plata, admiring its old Victorian-style mansions. Our tour guide took us to the Brugal rum factory, one of the biggest in the country, showing us the distillery and the rum production process. We also visited the Amber Museum and I was unable to resist buying a beautiful amber necklace and earrings. We had wonderful weather and returned to Toronto well rested.

Our arrival in Toronto was late; it was almost midnight. When we opened the door of our apartment, Ami dashed toward us like a missile, showing his profound joy at our arrival by jumping at us, waving his tail and running back and forth. Mishko was sitting in the family room, looking at us with a somewhat strange expression. When we asked where Hana was, he said that she had something to do downtown. Then, Mishko announced that Hana had given birth prematurely to healthy twin boys. I thought I had understood wrongly, but no, he had just been trying to keep it a surprise until Hana called. We were thrilled. The babies were healthy, which was a blessing. Hana had a slight infection but was already feeling better. Then the phone rang – it was our new mother calling from Mount Sinai Hospital. We asked why they hadn't called to tell us the big news; they said that they knew we would have returned right away, which they didn't want us to do.

Because Hana was not yet allowed to walk, Mishko was taking care of the boys, who were in incubators. They were born five minutes apart on April 28, 1985. The older was named Yair, the younger Daniel. We call them Yarko and Danielko. They were beautiful. On weekends, we went to their house or they came to us. When we laid the boys down on blankets on the floor, Ami sat at their heads and stood guard. He was very patient and never even licked them.

Not long after the babies were born, we received a letter from Ivo, Peter and Micka's younger son, telling us that he, his wife, Iveta, and daughter, Dominika, had fled Czechoslovakia for Vienna and intended to immigrate to Canada. We were, of course, willing to help them. We wrote a letter to Immigration Canada stating that the family was being sponsored by the Czechoslovak National Association in Canada and that we would gladly support them as co-sponsors. We asked the authorities to allow the family to come to Canada as soon as possible.

Paul and Mišhko decided to meet them in Vienna. I took some time off work and met Hana and the babies every day. We usually sat in the park behind the Art Gallery of Ontario or took a stroll on Queen and Bathurst streets. We often met the same "street people," whose faces broadened with smiles when they looked into the carriage and talked to our little babies. I wondered if they might have been reminded of their own children, when they were still living a normal life. Through my work I was frequently in touch with such unfortunate people, who lived on the street or in hostels and were alcoholics or on drugs. I know that sometime in an earlier life they had been teachers, entertainers, some of them well educated. Then, something tragic had happened to pull them down and they fell so far that there was no possible way to get up again.

Paul and Mišhko spent a few days in Frankfurt, Germany with Paul's cousin Palko and his family and later went to Vienna to meet Ivo. They returned to Toronto within two weeks and Ivo and his family arrived in early fall. They stayed with our children, which was an enormous help as they could share household expenses. Dominika, a very cute little girl, was five years old.

As most immigrants do in the beginning, Ivo worked at odd jobs. After a while, when his English was more polished, we managed to arrange an interview for him at Citytv and they hired him as a cameraman. Iveta was an engineer in a specialized field of fine optics. She took an English course and when she finished it, found a job in her profession. Unfortunately, though, Ivo and Iveta weren't doing well together, which had apparently started before they came to

Canada, and eventually they divorced. This had a terrible impact on Dominika at the time, but fortunately she adjusted and grew into a happy child. Ivo later met a divorced woman named Lenka. She was of Czech origin, a few years older than Ivo, and had a daughter, Linda, who was six years older than Dominika. It was the best thing that could have happened for Dominika, maybe for both of them. The two girls became very close, like sisters. It was magic and their relationship has lasted to this day.

~

In 1986, when the national office of the Canadian Red Cross moved to Ottawa, I felt fortunate to have taken the job at the Toronto branch – I didn't have to decide whether to look for another job in Toronto or move to Ottawa. At the same time, the Ontario Division had decided to move to Mississauga, so the Toronto Branch had to vacate the building, which had been sold. In November 1987 we moved into a small, fairly new three-storey building, on Yonge Street, just north of St. Clair Avenue.

In 1987, Miško and Hana decided to leave Toronto for Jerusalem. The children were over two years old, healthy and beautiful. Paul and I were quite unhappy about their departure but there was nothing we could do. It was their life.

Coping with Loss

In the summer of 1988, Paul and I decided to go on a two-week cruise in Greece. There had been a terrorist attack on a plane landing at the airport in Athens in 1986, but that kind of thing had never held us back from travelling anywhere, including Israel, where attacks were taking place on a regular basis. If we worried about things like this, we wouldn't have travelled anywhere. There is no safe place on earth any more.

We flew to Athens and then went by taxi to the port of Piraeus, where we boarded a massive ship, the *Pegasus*, part of the Epirotiki lines. We had a quite comfortable room with an ocean view and the ship was filled with all sorts of entertainment, including a casino, a disco and a cinema. The ship took four days to travel to the island of Rhodes, where we stayed for one week in the spectacular, modern Olympic Palace hotel with an ocean view. We strolled through the old city surrounded by medieval walls, enjoyed outdoor coffeehouses and browsed modern shops in the new town. In a fur store we bought our grandchildren cute little sheepskin vests.

We visited the Acropolis located on the side of Monte Smith's Hill, from which we had a spectacular panoramic view of the old and new towns and the restored ancient stadium. The fifth day we again boarded the ship and sailed to the islands of Mykonos, Santorini, Crete and Patmos. The buildings and villas of white stone make a dazzling contrast with the blue sky and clear, blue ocean. Santorini, in my eyes, was the most spectacular; it is actually the rim of an ancient volcano. There is a cable car to the top, where a village had been built, or one could take a donkey ride. I didn't trust the donkeys at all, seeing them staring stupidly at the wall. I just could not see myself sitting on a donkey, swaying from one side to the other as we climbed up such a steep height that practically hung over the ocean. The cable car seemed less frightening, but hanging over the ocean in it was both breathtaking and nerve-wracking.

Our next destination was the Turkish port of Kusadasi, which is lined on both sides of the street with stores carrying leather goods and Persian carpets. After some shopping, we were taken by bus to Ephesus, the tenth-century B C E city that is the largest excavated area in the world. It was interesting walking among these ruins, reading signs where the library, the church and the house with prostitutes had been. According to our guide, men going to visit the house of prostitution usually told their wives that they were going to the library, which was on the way. Further along we came to the huge stone amphitheatre, where we took a rest overlooking the land, the hills and the valley below us.

We sailed back to Patmos, where we took a three-hour break to visit the grotto where St. John wrote his book. Back in Athens, our hotel's splendid location enabled us to walk through a lovely park to the famous Athens museum and our window had a lovely view at night of the Acropolis all lit up. We went to see it the next day and strolled through the Plaka neighbourhood in the old city.

We returned home ready to start work and enjoy our lovely home, but when Paul came home from a checkup with our family doctor, he found out that the glands on the left side of his neck were swollen. The biopsy proved to be negative, but the oncologist was unwilling to make a judgment and left it to Paul whether to do exploratory surgery. He decided to operate and the doctors found cancer, non-Hodgkin's lymphoma. The surgeon suggested chemotherapy and to my surprise recommended that I explain the situation to Paul and try to convince him to undergo chemotherapy. It is difficult for me even now to explain my feelings. I was afraid of the future, yet I knew that I had to be the strong one.

When Paul started coming out of the anesthesia, I dreaded having to give him the bad news. I was sitting on a chair next to his bed when he was conscious enough to ask what the surgeon had found. I told him as gently as I could. Was he angry? Was he fearful? Or both? He didn't say anything for a long time. I tried to give him as much hope as I could, telling him that he had to undergo chemotherapy. He didn't want to hear about it. I begged him, saying how important it was to ensure his recovery. Finally, he consented and from that moment on he was the bravest I have ever known him. He believed in getting well and never complained.

Whenever I asked him how he felt, he always answered, "Okay." He lost his hair, but that didn't matter. At work, my bosses were understanding and allowed me to join Paul at the hospital every week. I would sit next to him when he got the therapy, and Ivo would drive us home. Paul always slept after the treatment but I had to wake him up every hour to give him liquids. I was under a lot of stress but the main goal was Paul's full recovery.

Eventually, Paul was able to go back to work. We were so lucky! Within a few months, Paul started to look well, his normally thin hair grew back and he felt fine. The oncologist proclaimed his condition to be in remission. No one who has not gone through this experience can understand how grateful we were to be given another lease on his life.

After Paul's terrible health scare, we heard that a World Rally of Czechoslovak Jews was going to be held in Israel from April 26 to May 5, 1990. Paul was feeling and looking well; he wanted to go and I gladly agreed. The festive opening of the World Rally took place in the huge convention centre Binyenei HaUma in Jerusalem under the patronage of Robert Maxwell, President Chaim Herzog of Israel,

Mayor Teddy Kollek of Jerusalem, and President Václav Havel of Czechoslovakia.

I think that everyone must have had a special feeling about this extraordinary event; some may have even been quietly hoping for reunions with family or friends. It was a once-in-a-lifetime occasion. For the first time since World War ii, Czech Jews gathered from all over the world. Different programs were planned every day and buses took people to visit many places. There were lectures on various subjects by academics from other countries; organized, round trips to kibbutzim; special sports, religious or war veterans meetings; and excursions to the historical parts of Jerusalem and other cities. The agenda was packed with interesting events and it was hard to choose which program to attend.

Paul and I felt a little guilty when we came home after a long day to spend time with our children. They quietly expressed their feelings about rarely seeing us by greeting us with, "Welcome to the Solan hotel." We knew that it was only partly a joke. Tickets to the events were hard to obtain, but we once managed a ticket for Miško and another time for Hana. We wanted them to experience the special atmosphere there, the rare moments when people met after so many years, sometimes not even knowing that these people were alive. We, for example, reconnected with Stefan Lucky, whom we had met at the Austrian border when leaving Czechoslovakia; he was still living in Prague. We were also delighted that the Schönfelds came from Tel Aviv and joined us for most of the programs.

The farewell party with dinner took place in Kfar Maccabiah in Ramat Gan. We arrived about two hours before dinner and mingled with people in the beautiful garden. Everyone had a name tag – the women's tags included their maiden names, as well as people's original surnames if they had changed them. They also indicated their present home countries. I spoke to a woman about my age whom I remembered from Theresienstadt because of her strong, characteristic physical features. She was living in a town in the north of Israel and led me to a group of people so that she could introduce me to her husband. When she stopped at the group where Paul was standing with other friends of ours, I was astonished. It turns out that her husband was originally from Banská Bystrica. What a small world it is. We met Paul's cousin and family from Germany and countless other friends from Toronto, including the "small" Věra with her husband, Karol. It was an extraordinary evening, impossible to forget.

⁓

That New Year's eve, in Toronto, we filled our champagne glasses and waited for the gong to announce the beginning of 1991. Our friends all wished one another the best for a good year ahead, better than the last one. A couple of weeks later, on January 17, 1991, the start of a war in the Persian Gulf was in the hands of US President George W. H. Bush and the coalition leaders. The deadline for Iraq's withdrawal from Kuwait had passed with Baghdad maintaining its defiance as the countdown to war began. Saddam Hussein had taken over direct command of the Iraqi army and assured his people and the rest of the world that his troops were ready to fight.

Air strikes were launched to drive Hussein's army from Kuwait and President Bush announced the commencement of Operation Desert Storm, the US code name for the Gulf War. Desert Storm included air attacks intended to destroy Iraq's nuclear weapons potential and chemical weapons stock, as well as damage tank forces.

In Canada, however, life went on. We were invited to a bat mitzvah that same day, January 17, 1991. The ceremony was at 9:00 a.m., followed by a luncheon and evening party to celebrate the girl's twelfth birthday and her becoming a woman. The synagogue was heavily guarded by police because there were threats of terrorism by Saddam Hussein against the allied countries. It gave me a feeling of being protected; Jewish people, especially, were alert. The entrance hall was crowded, with some people chatting about the latest attacks and strategies, others admiring the bat mitzvah girl.

It was a lavish affair and as the evening progressed, the mood was joyous. People danced the hora and the girl's friends lifted her into the air on a chair, as is the custom. At times, the orchestra banged its rhythm into a wild, spontaneous dance, and the air was filled with excitement; at the tables people ended with a wild rotation of hands, waving their napkins in circles above their heads. Paul and I didn't fit into this cheerful atmosphere. We felt sad, our thoughts with our loved ones and with the people of Israel who once again were expecting harsh times and aggression. We aren't religious, but try to respect and protect the Jewish way of life with dignity and human understanding.

After this event, we were all glued to the television, night and day. The coalition stepped up their bombing, accusing Baghdad of atrocities against the Kuwaiti people. Iraqi missiles pounded Israel. Thanks to the US president and congress, the US army was sent to Israel with their sophisticated weaponry, helping to dispose of the missiles. For the first time in our lives we could see, in detail, war unfolding on the TV screen. It was frightening. There was a danger that Saddam would use chemical weapons on Israel. For weeks, Israeli citizens were fully prepared for such attacks, sitting in one room of their homes, windows and walls covered with nylon protective covers, with gas masks and supplies of food and drinks, prepared for the worst.

No one went to work; no child went to school. One of the shocking, but also admirable, images on TV was a concert hall in Tel Aviv where the music of Beethoven was played and the entire audience, including the musicians and the conductor, wore gas masks. It looked tragically grotesque, but what spirit these people had, tested again and again and showing nothing but intrepid resistance.

Once the ground war began, the Iraqi army surrendered. As the war ended, on February 28, 1991, Iraqi forces set hundreds of Kuwait's oil wells ablaze. Troops gradually came home and were given a heroes' welcome by ecstatic crowds of spouses, parents, friends, lovers and children.

Paul's sixty-seventh birthday, on March 9, was nearing. I couldn't make a surprise party for him because he never liked being the centre of attention. He was too shy. He was well-liked among our friends and his colleagues as he was always willing to help where he could. He was a very generous individual. Instead of a surprise party, I invited about five couples with whom we usually celebrated our birthdays. That was the number that Paul could easily handle and we had a pleasant evening.

Three days after the party, however, Paul got sick with a high fever. I expected it to be the flu but the flu symptoms didn't really develop. In a few days the fever dropped, but it lingered at a decreased temperature for a longer time. I had to insist that he go to see the doctor because he was seldom willing to do so. The news was disastrous – there was a relapse of the cancer. In a short period of time he lost weight, became more fatigued and experienced a loss of appetite. Because the relapse was so rapid, the oncologist first thought it was an aggressive form of lymphoma. Numerous tests revealed the disease was greatly exacerbated, now involving the rapidly enlarging spleen and spilling over into the peripheral bloodstream to give rise to leukemia. A bone marrow test was carried out with a combination of oral treatments.

This was nothing comparable to Paul's first state of sickness. It was devastating. Nevertheless, even in such a state of illness, he continued to stay in touch with the people in the stores he was responsible for. He gave advice over the telephone and dictated the shift schedules to me so I could fax them to the bakery.

I asked Mišhko to come and he stayed for about three weeks. Having him there was easier for me because he could drive the car to and from the hospital. He could also spend time with his father, whom I was not sure he would have for much longer. Paul got excellent care in Mount Sinai Hospital. He got every treatment possible and was seen by every physician they thought could help. Paul knew every nurse's name; he used his old charm on them and they liked him very much. Friends and colleagues visited him on a regular basis, as did Ivo and Lenka, which we so appreciated. Sometimes, however, I had to remind some of them to leave because long visits were too exhausting for Paul. As a result of his various medications, Paul's good-natured disposition changed and he was often irritable, sometimes even aggressive. Mishko was unable to deal with this and it wasn't easy for me either, but at least I could understand and be patient, knowing that he wasn't quite himself anymore.

Paul phoned me from the hospital in the early morning before I went to work and after work I went straight to the hospital, caring for his personal hygiene, sitting next to him, talking, holding hands or letting him rest. When Paul was finally able to be at home, Ivo did the heavy task of carrying Paul into the bathroom and giving him a bath. Paul no longer had the strength to walk.

As soon as Paul mentioned that he would like a certain meal, I immediately started cooking, but when I offered it, he rarely touched it. The prognosis for any recovery got less and less promising. His body became nothing but skin and bones. My optimistic nature started to dissolve into quiet despair. While I tried to block out any possibility of losing him, our family doctor tried to prepare me for the worst.

Since I still had to work, I thought that I would get home care, a trained person who would be able to take care of Paul during my absence. Paul, however, was stubborn and dismissed the idea; he absolutely did not want to have anyone around except me. I didn't care that it was hard for me physically as well as mentally. I was exhausted but I was like a robot; every day, I discovered energy that I never knew I had. I was grateful for it. I got up at 5:30 every morning, prepared all his meals to be later warmed up in the microwave, then organized all his medication and put it on his bed table. Before I left for work I washed him, taking complete care to see that he always looked presentable. Laci, a friend who lived in the building, had a key to our apartment so he could check on him.

I once got a call at the office from my friend Nushi to come home immediately because Laci had found Paul lying on the floor next to the bed. It was a miracle that Paul wasn't hurt. I could see that it was a hazard to leave him alone at home, but he still wasn't willing to have a stranger around him. What was the solution? I suggested that I take some leave from the office for three weeks, working half-days only. Paul seemed pleased with the idea and my office agreed. No other mishaps occurred.

Then Paul practically stopped eating. I was alarmed and knew that he needed hospital care to receive intravenous nutrition. When I told him that I needed to call an ambulance, however, Paul said that if the paramedics came, he would refuse to go. Not wanting to take responsibility for him starving to death, I called the ambulance anyway. The attendants were wonderful. They admired our house and our paintings, which softened Paul enough to let him think reasonably. Perhaps he was afraid that he would be seeing his apartment for the last time.

The Schönfelds came from Israel, which made Paul very happy. Luci, who had been friends with him since childhood, spent most of her time with him.

In hospital, Paul received numerous blood transfusions, which were hard on him. Then the day came that he just couldn't get warm – covering him with blankets didn't seem to help. Years ago, before he got sick, we discussed at length that if either of us suffered a serious illness, we did not want to be put on life support, hooked up to machines. Our family doctor had that statement on file. When two young doctors came into Paul's room and started asking him about his wishes regarding possible resuscitation, I heard him ask if things had come that far already. They answered that it was their policy to have his wishes in writing for future reference. Paul told them that they should do whatever possible to keep him alive.

By this time, his condition was so serious that one organ after the other started to slowly fail. He was hooked to oxygen because at times not enough oxygen was getting to his brain, which sometimes led to him to give vague, even unclear answers. My opinion is that in this situation, policy or no policy, it was not fair to ask such questions. I translated the questions into his mother tongue, but his answers were always the same. As a result, what happened was the opposite of what we had always talked about when we were still in good health.

Paul was having difficulty breathing. I was standing next to him, holding his hand, feeling that his life was coming to its end. I didn't want him to suffer. He had been such an active individual and with so many impediments, life was not a gift anymore. With my hand in his, I felt his last breath. I knew it was the best for him. I called the nurse and the doctor came to confirm his death. It was August 2, 1991.

We phoned Mishko to take the next flight to Toronto and he arrived the next day. Quite a few years ago, Paul and I had discussed that we would both want to be cremated. He wanted a simple, dignified ceremony with our favourite music. We didn't want a rabbi. We were both agnostic and would not settle for any insincere act. After looking around, Paul and I had decided on Mount Pleasant Cemetery, right in the middle of the city. It is a huge and wonderfully kept park with many rare trees. We chose the colour of marble we wanted for covering the urns in the soil.

My nephew Ivo and his wife, Lenka, went with me to make funeral arrangements. Luci Schönfeld and Lenka helped me to choose a black dress. We also ordered the flower arrangements. I functioned in a mechanical way. I made the list of relatives and friends to be informed; we phoned friends to invite them to the funeral; I ordered announcements to be sent out by mail to other towns and countries. I was amazed at how I could take part in these chores, but I did. I was in a kind of daze, surrounded by people. We were all busy. Mishko helped me to go through the necessary documents for future dealings with the government. He decided to stay with me for one month.

It was the first time in my life I took sleeping pills. It was just horrible to wake up in the morning, realizing that Paul was never going to be with us anymore.

Miško and Ivo prepared the music – songs by Gershwin, "The Man I Love," and the melodies by Nat King Cole that Paul had loved to listen to. They also prepared photographs of him and of us together for display. We arranged to have the largest hall for the ceremony and it was packed with our colleagues and friends. Paul's Aunt Aranka came from New York; his cousin Steve came from Boston with his wife; my cousin Karl and his wife, Emmy, came from Montreal; Juca Schanzer came from Ottawa. Two of our friends gave moving eulogies. The ceremony was simple and dignified. After the funeral, we served refreshments donated by the Open Window Bakery in our apartment.

Slowly I began to respond to the nearly one hundred sympathy wishes. Then after one week, I returned to my somewhat normal routine, swimming in the morning, followed by work, which was my salvation. I was fully involved in my clients' problems and didn't have time to think about myself.

My complete loss had not sunk in yet. I couldn't listen to any kind of music. I was more comfortable when it was raining or cloudy. I hardly could stand the bright sun. I was filled with pain and sadness. I didn't want to hear anyone laughing. I have never, never been envious in my whole life but when I saw an elderly couple holding hands on the street, I envied them.

Miško was compassionate. At some point, he started quietly playing a CD of the "Unfinished Symphony" by Franz Schubert, which he knew I loved. I came into the room and listened. He understood that I had to be gently pushed into action. Then, the day came that he had to leave. I knew very well that life had to go on.

Five months went by and I felt an immense emptiness. I had always loved to read but I couldn't concentrate. I was grateful for any voice on the radio or TV, which I immediately turned on when I came home. And again, when I opened my eyes in the morning, there was my little radio, still tuned to the station Paul had listened to.

One morning I heard the voice of Nat King Cole, with his daughter Natalie, singing, "Unforgettable, that's what you are." Yes, I thought, that's what you are. That evening, when I went to bed, I turned over to touch his hand and I wanted him back.

We were together for forty-five years. We had a good relationship, at times rocky, but we both loved each other very much and that is why we stayed together. We were so close that sometimes we could read each other's minds. He was caring and considerate. He always brought me flowers or other presents to show that I was in his mind and heart.

Two of my friends made the remark that it is more painful if someone dies unexpectedly, when it comes as a shock, and I thought to myself, how do they know? Both of their husbands were still alive. Watching a loved one deteriorating from one day to the other was very painful, feeling both helpless and in denial about the seriousness of the situation.

One of our acquaintances who was widowed about the same time as me committed suicide. She had grown children living in Toronto. I often heard people saying that she shouldn't have done it. Who are we to judge a person? If she was that desperate in her misery and found the courage to carry it out, then now she is at peace. I wouldn't have attempted anything like that, but losing a loved one is such an enormous adjustment. It takes a lot of time and optimism to adjust. There is no one who will stroke your hair or hold your hand. There is no one left to talk to about the most intimate things. I was glad to have had the luxury to be by myself, free to cry until my tears lulled me to sleep.

When one becomes a widow (what an ugly word), everyone wants to be your friend for about three months, then you are on your own. It is not that people stop caring – they just need to get on with their own lives. If I hadn't had a few close, single friends, my weekends would have been miserably lonely. The exceptions were parties, to which I was still invited and which I appreciated. After a few months,

I started laughing at a joke someone told at a party. At the time, I was stricken by my conduct, but soon I realized that life goes on and even I had to come to grips with the situation.

I started to put my thoughts in writing while I was sitting on the train or bus on my way to or from work. I found it therapeutic and it gave me peace of mind. That is when I decided to continue writing an autobiography for my son and grandchildren.

On My Own

Shortly after Paul died, Peter asked me to come to Bratislava to settle some legal matters with regard to property there. There were a number of reasons I couldn't go. In the first place, I had to arrange my pensions with the government here, which was vital to making certain I had some income.

Secondly, I was not mentally prepared to deal with such matters and face either my relatives or other people. Many individuals don't understand that after the death of a loved one, there is a grieving process that is absolutely necessary to go through. It can last a long time. I often still see Paul in my dreams; I can never forget him – with both his faults and kindness, I loved him very much.

Exactly one year later I suddenly felt that the time had come for me to prepare for the trip. It was the first time that I had had to arrange everything with my travel agent for the trip to Prague, Bratislava and Israel. I planned to stay out of Canada for a little over one month. I still didn't want to see many people, just Věra and Laco in Prague, Peter and Micka in Bratislava, the children in Jerusalem and Luci in Tel Aviv.

It was also the first time that I had sat in a plane by myself. It felt strange and would be the first of many first times for me on my own. By the time the plane was about to land in Prague, I was excited about seeing the Zemans. As soon as I saw them, we embraced and kissed; we were so happy to see each other. The following days went by like a dream. We hardly stopped talking. I felt lucky to have such wonderful friends.

Seeing Peter and Micka was very emotional. We have always had a wonderful relationship and Micka and I were close friends through the years. We went to the theatre; we walked and talked about many things. We watched television in the evenings, including programs from Austria, which I especially appreciated. We also took a trip to Komárno where Micka's mother lived. She was a woman in her late eighties, living in her own house and handling things all by herself. On top of it, she was still teaching German to private students. She was still attractive and had just a few wrinkles on her face; her brown eyes sparkled and she was always smiling.

When it was time for me to leave, Micka and Peter drove me to the airport, where I would board an El Al flight to Israel. We had a touching farewell and I was off to the gate. I later found out that, for safety reasons, the El Al counter had no sign. It was visible only by heavily armed personnel, two men with machine guns. I found my way to the area where we were to have a strict personal and luggage inspection. A few young women walked back and forth through the corridor with walkie-talkies.

When I was through the inspection, I took a seat on a bench next to a lady from Vienna who spoke German and we started talking about Vienna. She was pleased that I knew the city. We were supposed to board the plane a half an hour earlier and I wondered why it was taking so long. The lady suggested that the reason might be the disaster that had occurred the day before. I looked surprised as she mentioned that a plane had crashed over Holland, leaving quite a few casualties. She couldn't recall the last time anything like this had happened to an El Al plane. Then I realized why Peter and Micka had not been listening to the radio as usual. They hadn't wanted me to worry.

A few minutes later, the loudspeaker announced that we should line up to board the bus for the plane, which had been carefully checked out for any suspicious packages.

Our landing at Ben Gurion Airport was delayed an hour. I spotted Mišhko right away, along with my two grandsons and Luci. I usually try to be a reasonable grandmother and not brag too much, but I have to say that their features are unusually beautiful. We went to the airport cafeteria and sat down for a snack and a drink to discuss when I would visit Luci, as she wanted me to stay for a few days. Mišhko suggested the last few days of my visit, which suited Luci well because she wanted to take me to the airport, located between Jerusalem and Tel Aviv but a little closer to Kir'on, where Luci lived.

The weather was warm, with a pleasant light breeze. The children lived in a condominium in a residential area on the outskirts of Jerusalem, in a fairly new three-storey building. They made me comfortable in their bedroom and moved into the living room. During my stay I tried to cook and bake as much as I could, knowing that my cooking is different from their Arabic-Jewish style. I think the change was very much appreciated. The boys were extremely active; I always wonder about so much energy concentrated in such skinny little bodies. They played football in the nearby park; they went cycling; and they had just taken up judo, at which they really excelled.

I wasn't in the mood to socialize but I did call Rolland Černy's son Ron in Tel Aviv. Unfortunately he couldn't visit us because he was just leaving for a business trip. My stays with Luci are usually so pleasant but this time, it was hard for both of us. Vilko had died of pancreatic cancer half a year after Paul passed away. We talked about them and felt that it was a healing process. It was so good to reminisce until we fell asleep. Shortly before Vilko died, he had written me a letter explaining his health condition and other personal matters. I gave Luci the letter; I knew how much she would treasure it.

Luci has nine grandchildren. The ones who are Yarko and Daniel's age and lived around the corner came to play when my grandchildren were visiting. Her two daughters, Eva and Hana, also came with their husbands and then there was a full house. Mishko practically grew up with Eva and Hana in Prague and we knew Hana's husband, Kaja, when he was a little boy because he was the son of our mutual friends, the Edlans.

My daughter-in-law, Hana, was a director of a special school with an experimental program – my grandchildren attended the school. One of the specialties was an intense focus on the students' various abilities and talents. They are evaluated individually in front of their parents and their teacher. Hana is a successful professional and since he wasn't working, Michal took care of the children and the household. Unfortunately, their relationship deteriorated and they both needed a separation, so in 1994, Mishko came to Canada to stay with me. He had to sort things out in a different situation. My friend Susi, who was the bookkeeper in a large electronic company not far from us, arranged for Mishko to get a job in the warehouse. I was glad about it. He needed a normal life, time and the opportunity to be alone. A physical job was exactly what he needed for the time being.

Although the time we spent together was not easy for either of us, my apartment was big enough to allow us each some privacy. I tried to be both tactful and helpful to him. It was also difficult for me. But I am the mother and the only one he could lean on. I had to be there for him.

Mishko finally decided that he had to go back; he wanted to live with his children. Yarko and Daniel were having a hard time without their father and they were also afraid that he would not come back. After eight months in Toronto, he was ready to go. He seemed to be in good spirits, even optimistic about putting his life together. I was worried about him until he, thankfully, found a job. A burden fell from my heart and I convinced myself, as I had many times before, that there are always better times ahead of us.

～

At the end of 1994, I was nearing retirement. Since my birthday is in December, I was supposed to work until the end of the month and retire in January 1995. I was so fortunate to have been given the opportunity of working in International Services. After years of experience, I had reached a high level of professionalism in this field. I truly loved the work, which contributed to my success. I think that my clients must have felt my interest, as I constantly followed up cases, insisting that colleagues working on them strive for positive results. In my spare time my thoughts often drifted to some especially difficult tracing cases, trying to figure out how to proceed from the dead end I had encountered. A reunion of two people or a family was a celebration for me as well as for the individuals involved.

Our office had settled into our new place on Yonge Street. It was cozy, with only about forty people in the whole building. Times are always changing, though, and so are work places. The national office announced an upcoming reorganization and new policies that were distressing for some employees. New job descriptions resulted in an amalgamation of functions for the same salary and all the metro Toronto branches were replaced by a regional office that would have authority over suburban community offices.

In addition to those changes, the board of directors and senior administration had decided to declare that all jobs, except mine, would be subject to a competition. I was the only one allowed to keep my job unless I preferred to compete for another. I was stunned and pleased, realizing that I had such an exceptional choice. I decided to keep my job until my retirement; I wasn't really interested in pursuing a different type of work and leaving what I had lovingly built up for years.

Nonetheless, my job did change into a teaching and guiding position. I had to hold regular workshops for five community offices, teaching the staff about the work of the international services and how to conduct investigations. I enjoyed the teaching part, but I was sorry to give up the investigative work that had given me so much pleasure. I had to delegate inquiries to the community offices, knowing that it took years of experience to learn all the nuances of investigating. I did the best I could, but I started to count the days to retirement and didn't make any secret of it. I was preparing for another era of my life, one in which I could do things I had never had time for while I was working.

One day, Ginny, my immediate boss, said to me, "Reserve December 14 after work. Dress up, but don't ask me anything more." I knew that there would be a retirement party for me but they kept it from me well; I was not even told the location. A colleague of mine, Dennis, drove me downtown and stopped in front of the King Edward Hotel. Inside, he led me to the Variety Club Room, which was full of people sitting around tables, all familiar faces I had worked with, including colleagues from the community offices and some from the Ontario division. Dennis pinned a corsage on my evening jacket lapel, whispering that he didn't know which way was up and which was down. I couldn't resist answering, "What a shame! You should know that!" and we both burst out laughing. Thus we made our happy entrance.

To my amazement, my eye caught a table of my closest friends. I wondered how Mary, our secretary, had found out their names and addresses, then reminded myself that she also worked in the "Sherlock Holmes" department. I was touched. Sitting there were Nushi with Zoli, Agi with Shani (Alex), Hana with John, and volunteers John, Grace, Theresa and Georgina. Our previous executive director and his wife were also present, as well as many people I really did not expect but I felt honoured that they had come. Ginny took me to the bar and ordered me a shot of vodka, which was quite a clever thought. I moved from one table to another, chatting with everyone.

After dinner, the formal part of the evening began. Millie from the Ontario division gave her speech, as did Donna from our office. On behalf of the volunteers, John read from a long, long list of wonderful poems he had composed. The paper was folded and reached the floor, giving the impression that he would read for a long time, but the paper was mostly blank. It was very funny. The commissioner of the Ontario division had sent me a wonderful letter in appreciation of my long commitment and dedication to the service of the Red Cross. I was flattered and felt a little vain, but I was happy to hear the compliments on my past performance at the organization.

Then it was my turn. I talked about the beginnings, mentioning how lucky I was to have worked in a field I loved, and thanked every person, especially Donna, Christine and Ginny, for their understanding and humanity during the time Paul was so ill. I received a beautiful flower arrangement, an envelope with a monetary gift and many other presents, including a bottle of vodka. We had a ball and left late that night.

After my retirement, I looked around to see what kind of special programs the city offered free for seniors. Every Friday there were lectures for seniors at the Art Gallery of Ontario, so Nushi and I went to try it out. Volunteer guides led us through a display of paintings, drawings and sculptures, teaching us about artists and their backgrounds, comparing their styles with those of other artists. These lectures are a wonderful way to experience the joy and beauty of art, which sometimes move me to tears.

Another time, I went to the Glenn Gould studio at the CBC building, where Sunday's radio music programs are taped and where some of the most talented musicians have the opportunity to entertain the public. I listened to Sir Michael Tippett's "The Blue Guitar" (inspired by Picasso's painting, "The Old Guitarist"), his sonata for four horns and piano sonata No. 2. I was amazed. It sounded like atonal music to me, wails and high-pitched cries in a nightmare. I closed my eyes and pictured a horrific experience like hanging on a high wall, agonizingly afraid of falling into a deep wild river below or haunted by huge creatures in a dark forest. I wondered if the composer might have gone through a fearful experience and was expressing his feelings through music. What pain and fear had made this man express his passion by composing such music? The experience was both incredible and interesting. I consider myself blessed to be able to explore different kinds of art, no matter whether it is to my taste or not. My curiosity to learn is greater than ever and I always want to look deeper into a piece of art, trying to understand the artist's intention.

I also went to the Summer Jazz Festival sponsored by the du Maurier Tobacco Company. I always used to go with Paul. The good old melodies elevated my spirits. The US Field Band played Dixieland, Glenn Miller, Count Basie and Benny Goodman. That was the music of our youth. I felt as though Paul were close to me; it was just magic. When I don't have a program or event planned, I like to simply stroll through the city. I am free to decide where to go and to discover new places. There is always something of interest to catch my eye and my attention.

I have always relied more on the public transit system than on a car. Paul always needed his car for work so I used the bus and subway. When Paul died, I sold the car. I always liked the subway system and there are usually taxis around. In a car you are isolated, but in the bus or subway, you may observe people. You can feel the atmosphere of the place. When I am not reading, I sometimes admire all the different people I see. There is so much international diversity and some people are dressed in the style of their own culture. This is one of the reasons that I love Canada, for the mosaic of nations, the multiculturalism.

Being retired, I had no special obligations in Toronto and for the second time in my life, I started planning a three-month vacation, making my own decisions. After arranging my itinerary with Miško and the friends I wanted to visit, I decided that I would spend three weeks in Prague staying with Věra and Laco, another three weeks in Bratislava with Micka and Peter and the rest of the time with Miško and the children in Jerusalem. Also included was a few days with Luci. I was looking forward to the Zemans' plan to spend a week with their grandchildren at a cottage in Šumava, a lovely mountainous area of the Czech Republic.

The Zemans met me at the airport and we drove through the lovely part of Prague – around the castle from the hill down, opening with the view of the bridges over the Vltava River, looking at the surrounding spires of churches, towers of historical houses and buildings. I had forgotten how truly exquisite the view is. We chatted, reminiscing about old times, discussing the changes in the new political system, its frustrations, weaknesses and hopes.

Every day, we strolled through the city for hours. We both enjoyed it, but I was in heaven. I never stopped admiring the old city's urban style built from the tenth to the twentieth centuries, the city I was born in, lived in and knew like the palm of my hand. I love walking through the Lesser Side (Malá Strana), the old Jewish quarter, built up intensively in mature Gothic style overlooking the banks of the Vltava River, with the castle hill dominating the skyline and the later Renaissance buildings, especially the one from the Baroque period that molded the city in the second half of the seventeenth century into a brilliant architectural composition. I also took in the artistically groomed public gardens and sculptures, as well as the unique historical pavilions and belvederes surrounding old Prague.

We strolled through the old Coal Market with kiosks displaying fresh fruits, vegetables, flowers and gifts, often ending up at the Old Town Hall's astronomical clock, the Orloj, to look at the allegorical representations of the twelve months. Its revolving spheres not only show the hours of the day, the months and the years (even the leap years!), but also the movements of the planets, including the course of the sun and the moon. As the Old Town clock strikes the hour, a performance unfolds – two doors open and figurines representing the apostles and Death all move, one by one.

We left the city in the Zemans' old Škoda car in the early morning, travelling to the south of the Czech Republic. The landscape slowly changed, as we passed highways, dirt roads and villages, cottages traditionally built with painted beams, thatched roofs and little fenced gardens. I could see far ahead small houses with red roofs, fields of grain, green pastures with cows and horses. I listened to the bubble of the stream. The colour of deep, dark spruce and fir trees sometimes changed to a light green. The hills and mountains in the distance were still enveloped in haze. I closed my eyes, listening to the stillness, giving myself up to the tranquility of it all.

As soon as we reached our destination a little girl ran toward us. For a few seconds, I was back almost fifty years. What a startling resemblance she had to her mother, Hana, as a kid. She was adorable, with huge, sparkling black eyes and a big smile. We took to each other instantly. She was five years old and her older brother was eleven.

The view from the window in my room was splendid. The porch led into a yard with a garden filled with sunflowers, daisies, cornflowers and vegetable beds. We walked through the village and farther into the woods, picking mushrooms, blueberries and, on the way home, fresh flowers. Here and there we stopped at a porch or a farmyard to talk to friendly villagers. In the afternoons, we would often go for a swim in the pond. We walked up to the Javorník Mountain and made trips to neighbouring towns such as Sušice and Strakonice, and roamed through the old Raab Castle, which, as a remnant of the Communist regime, was still quite neglected.

There was time for reading and for quiet talks with Věra. The bond between us dates back fifty years to when we were in the concentration camp together; it was a shared experience impossible to compare with other relationships. There was also time for me to think, sitting on the porch looking into the blue sky, far away from the rush of a large city.

After a week, we returned to Prague where I met a few of my friends. One day, while I was sitting on a bench in the Franciscan garden, a hidden garden in the middle of Wenceslas Square, I became interested in listening to two senior citizens talk about the present political situation. The man complained that the Germans were again buying out Czech properties and businesses. They wondered in amazement how, after losing two wars, the Germans were able to recover so quickly economically as well as politically.

Many old establishments in Prague are gone or have moved. There is a noticeable excess of huge, elegant jewellery stores, but most of them don't have any customers. There are also new Chinese restaurants and the talk of the town is mafia involvement. Life in the city is intense. New business is booming, and new coffeehouses, snack bars, casinos, discos and entertainment attractions of all kinds have opened. There is a high spirit of enterprise. In 1995 the Czech Republic's annual inflation rate was 20 per cent and gross unemployment 5 per cent – prices were rising and many people needed to have two or three jobs to afford the daily necessities. Some businesses were flourishing, while others were going bankrupt. I wondered about the two men on the bench who complained of being on a small pension and could afford less than they did under the Communist regime. The Czech Republic has become a democratic country with a capitalist system, with the same ups and downs as many other countries.

The day came for me to say goodbye and I was on my way to Bratislava, where Peter and his nine-year-old grandson, Janko, were waiting for me. Micka had recently broken her arm and was in the hospital, so I stayed with Janko while Peter visited her. He was a quiet, smart, gentle boy and it was a pleasure to be with him.

Micka came home after four days with her arm in a cast, on a sling. She was limited in her movements, but we were there to help as much as we could. I always thought of Bratislava as a big village but there are so many cultural opportunities to enjoy. Micka could walk and wanted to show me the nice part of their city. We went downtown to galleries, museums and the presidential palace, which was open to the public and exhibiting paintings from the fifteenth to the eighteenth centuries, as well as sculptures, antique vases and ceramics.

After a wonderful trip to Bratislava, I stepped off the airplane in Israel. It is such a special feeling to land in that country. Many people say this. I am not religious, so I have no explanation for it, but it might be a feeling of belonging. Whatever it is, I always look forward to seeing my son, my grandchildren and Luci. Mishko borrowed a car and we drove toward Jerusalem. On the outskirts of the city, fireworks illuminated the sky, reminding everyone of the upcoming festivities to commemorate three thousand years since the founding of Jerusalem. As we entered the city, we were surrounded by festive decorations with various special flags and tropical plants.

It was a pleasantly warm September evening. Yarko and Daniel were then ten and a half years old; I intended on staying for five weeks and wanted to get to know them. We got along fine. Their English was at a beginner's level but what they did not understand, Mishko translated. They were mature enough to hold a serious conversation and it was usually after dinner that they started to question me about the Holocaust. They were fascinated by the topic. After a while I told them that I was writing my memoirs, which would be dedicated to their father and to both of them. They accepted this with satisfaction.

Quite a few times I was surprised by their questions, such as, "What kind of person are you?" I said, "You tell me what you think and we may discuss it further." And we did. They are bright children. We also laughed a lot. They were definitely surprised to see me spontaneously laugh to tears, which was always contagious. They loved it. We played games, I went with them into the nearby park and we took long walks. I helped them a bit with their English lessons and listened when Daniel played his flute and Yarko his violin. Yarko makes interesting sculptures and Daniel paints wonderfully; some of his paintings were displayed at school. Some of his works, which are rather abstract, I have framed and hung on the walls in my apartment.

The boys can be very appreciative. Most of the time, they loved my cooking and complimented me with a smile, saying how good it was. They loved to help me and were eager to assist with both cooking and setting the table. Daniel generously gave me his seat at the table, joining Yarko on the bench. The dear souls went shopping with me to the supermarket and patiently translated from Hebrew into English for me, suggesting what to buy. Under the bright sun in a temperature of thirty-five degrees Celsius, they helped me carry shopping bags home. When they asked me to read to them before bedtime, I gladly read from English *National Geographic* books that I had sent them. I once scolded them for being too wild with each other. When Miško came home from work and asked how their day was, the answer from both of them was, "Gerti was a little bit nervous today." One evening, they announced that I was wealthy. I told them that they were mistaken, that I am far from wealthy. Miško explained to me that they were not used to seeing a woman, especially a grandmother, wearing the latest fashion, having manicured red nails and changing her costume jewellery every day. They didn't know if it was real gold or not. I let them go through my jewellery box, explaining what I liked to wear. They showed me their treasures – the precious stones that they collect. We also spent some time with Hana. She invited all of us for dinner and, as I was there through the Jewish high holidays, we invited her for the second festive Rosh Hashanah holiday dinner.

Miško worked as a fundraiser for an organization called HaMoked, the Center for the Defence of the Individual, and he invited me to see his workplace. He took me around and introduced me to his colleagues. I talked to one young man who sits near Miško about his work, which is quite familiar to me. He initiates searches for Arab prisoners, finding out the location of their incarceration in order to inform the family of his or her location. There are also a few lawyers there. Miško introduced me to a young woman in her early thirties, named Rotem, whom he was dating. Her work consists of dealing with the government on behalf of separated Arab couples from the West Bank who wish to be reunited in Jerusalem. She is an anthropologist by profession and is very pleasant; Yarko and Daniel like her.

Jerusalem is a magnificent city. I had been there with Paul many times, once for a month, but there are always some new art buildings, mansions, colonnades and excavations I have not seen. I saw all kinds of dress – Hasidic capote, Muslim jalabiyas, dozens of different monk robes, people in jeans, people in modern European clothing, Arabs in their white robes, Orthodox Jewish women in dark dresses with simple hats. There were also groups of tourists and pilgrims.

The flora in Jerusalem is gorgeous. There are old oak trees, old birch trees and chestnut trees next to huge fir trees. Spruce trees grow next to tropical palm trees. The diversity was such a treat – I saw a pink, blooming fir tree whose top ended high up in the sky. Cactuses, planted in large pots, grace every balcony and porch. Miško and I relaxed on a stone bench in a garden in front of a bronze fountain with lions spitting out trickles of water. We walked to the Montefiore Windmill, built by Sir Moses Haim Montefiore, a British philanthropist of Jewish descent born in Italy in 1784. He devoted himself to improving the condition of Jews throughout the world and built the windmill in Jerusalem to give work to the poor and also provided them with housing quarters.

We also visited the recently finished Supreme Court neighbouring the Knesset (Israeli parliament), an important complex on a massive piece of land that incorporates all kinds of architectural elements. The Knesset itself is an interesting building of pink Jerusalem stone and faces a huge menorah presented to the Israelis by the British parliament. The interior has three magnificent tapestries hanging in the reception hall designed by artist Marc Chagall, who also did the floor and wall mosaics. We finished the excursion by passing through Sacher Park with its wide lawns, path of roses and duck pond surrounded by benches. Another striking complex dominates the new City Hall on Safra Square, built on an area covering 80,000 meters. It officially opened in 1993 and I am proud to acknowledge that it was built by a Canadian, architect Jack Diamond. Almost every day, I strolled through the downtown area among the many small art galleries, art shops, fashion stores and bookstores.

Years ago, with Paul, Hana, Miško and the children, I visited Yad

Vashem on the Mount of Remembrance, the monument to the six million European Jews murdered by Nazis during World War II. It features a simple and severe pillar rising seventy feet high into the sky. I only went to Yad Vashem once – I was afraid to reopen painful memories from the past. In the Children's Memorial Hall that commemorates the 1.5 million lost children, you walk in darkness under a blue ceiling covered with blinking stars, listening to the names of children who once lived in Europe. The names of twenty-two concentration and death camps are etched into the granite floor of the Memorial Hall. In the middle is the eternal flame. We walked through the Avenue of the Righteous Among the Nations, which honours the non-Jews who risked their lives trying to save their Jewish neighbours and friends. There are numerous monuments documenting the history of European Jews during the Nazi era. I was deeply touched and will never forget it.

Yad Vashem also has the propaganda film that the Nazis made in Theresienstadt. I knew that I was supposed to be in it, so we went to the office and asked if they could project it for us. I saw a short shot of my father's friend playing the violin in the orchestra, but I didn't see my father – he must have been sitting next to his friend. I also didn't see the movie I was in. The staff at Yad Vashem referred me to a kibbutz that might have it, but we didn't have enough time to travel there. Next time, I thought.

I twice stayed with my dear friend Luci for a few days in Tel Aviv. I am like her younger sister and she calls me *malička* (the little one). Broad-minded and generous, Luci is one of the kindest people I know. Whenever I stay with her I always find flowers and the finest chocolates on my bedside table. One or two pieces of her latest wardrobe are waiting for me and any kind of refusal is unthinkable.

We were invited for dinner at the home of one of her daughters. Both of Luci's sons-in-law are doctors and both are superb chefs. Hana's husband, Kaja, studied in Italy and knows how to make the best pasta in the world. The funny thing is that I am used to drinking vodka, but not wine. It got into my head a little and Luci and I had a really good time. Hana is a copy of Luci in looks. She paints, makes collages and illustrates books. She and Luci exhibited their work in an art gallery together. Hana has four beautiful daughters. Eva, on the other hand, studied drama and became an actress. Having had five children, however, she stayed at home for a few years and recently went back to teach drama at a school.

The next day, we met another friend originally from Banská Bystrica, Mató Galambos. We went to visit a very special place in Jaffa where, 250 years ago, pilgrims made their first stop in the Holy Land on their way to Jerusalem. Today's restored citadel of ancient Jaffa, the city's first hostel, has been transformed into a museum. It is named Ilana Goor, after the international designer, artist and sculptress who created this place full of sculptures, jewellery, old wood furniture, glass, bronze and iron. Facing the sea, overlooking the 4,000-year-old Jaffa port under the radiating sun, with the silhouettes of an ancient synagogue, minarets and church spires in the clear blue sky, I marvelled again at how many fascinating places there are in the world.

My stay in Israel slowly came to an end. I was glad to have made the trip; I loved every minute of it. I wanted to take a taxi by myself to the airport for my 2:00 a.m. flight, but Miško and the boys insisted on taking me. It was good to have them with me until the last minute. We kissed, embraced, and waved until they were out of sight. I was ready to go home.

Epilogue

Yarko and Daniel next came to visit me in the summer of 1996, when Hana, now my ex-daughter-in-law, was on sabbatical and decided to bring the boys to Toronto for almost three weeks. Less than a year earlier, on November 4, 1995, Yitzhak Rabin, the seventy-three-year-old prime minister of Israel and messenger of peace, had been assassinated. This political assassination shocked both Israelis and people around the world. Rabin died at the hands of an Israeli, a young Jewish law student named Yigal Amir. No Israeli could understand how one Jew could destroy another. Since that time, a strong wave of terrorism had re-entered Israel and I had been terrified when I called every weekend, afraid to get bad news. Each time, I was grateful for the news that my family was alive and unharmed. Miško said that Yair and Daniel were afraid to get on a bus because of recent attacks. I believe that everyone is afraid.

While my grandchildren were visiting, Hana phoned every day to arrange our time together. Sometimes we all went off together and sometimes she brought the boys in the morning so I could have them overnight and the next day. The boys loved to go swimming in our building and play ping-pong and billiards. Although Yarko and Daniel had always loved my cooking, how could I compete with McDonald's? As soon as they saw the sign, they asked if we could go. There was no sense in reasoning with them that we had dinner at home as they sounded in unison: "Please, please, let's go!" So I gave in.

August 2, 1996, was the fifth anniversary of Paul's death and the boys wanted to visit his grave. All four of us went to the cemetery. They bought flowers in a pot and placed them on the grave. They were quieter than usual and gently asked a lot of questions about him.

I was happy to have had the opportunity to get to know them better, although I was often exhausted during their visit. I had a wonderful time with them, though, and believe they enjoyed the stay in Toronto very much.

~

Since the last time I was in Prague, in the summer of 1995, Věra had had terrible coughing attacks. She was diagnosed with pulmonary fibrosis, a hereditary lung disease that her mother had died of in her early eighties. Through our correspondence, I knew that her condition had worsened. The five doctors in her family were at least making certain that she was suffering as little as possible. Then, on March 14, 1997, I got a letter from Laco saying that Věra had died. They had promised her that she would not suffocate, which was the only thing she was afraid of. Věra was only sixty-seven. These days, that is too young to die.

The pain of losing such a friend was intense. My thoughts were with her at night before I closed my eyes, as well as in the morning when I woke up. Laco was devastated. It will take a long time for him to recover. I unfortunately know the sorrow and suffering of losing a loved one. It never really goes away. It only began to ease for me about two years after it happened.

I am grateful for my present good health, but am I destined to keep experiencing the loss of my closest friends? What a price to pay! I have gone through many stages in my life. I have lost my loved ones. I have lost my possessions twice. It has made me stronger, made me achieve challenging goals, fortified me against the hardships of life.

I consider myself a lucky person. I lived with a man I loved. I have a healthy son who is a decent human being, and I have wonderful grandchildren. I find happiness in communicating with them and with my friends. I was privileged to work in such a rewarding field, finding dignity and generosity.

I am able to feel gratitude for each little thing I can do every day, enjoying both sunny and rainy days, going through small difficulties, finding satisfaction in being surrounded by art and devoting my free time to exercise. I am more of an agnostic than a believer. Through the years, I have come to the conclusion that to be a good human being and help people in a quiet way is important to me. I am content with having had a rich life and still expect to find something meaningful to get involved in.

Glossary

Ančerl, Karel (1908–1973) A renowned Czechoslovak conductor, Ančerl was the orchestra conductor for Prague radio between 1933 and 1939, until World War II interrupted broadcasting. In 1942, he and his family were deported to the Terezín ghetto, where Ančerl established the Terezín String Orchestra and organized musical performances. After the war, Ančerl continued to conduct for Prague radio, and in 1950 was appointed artistic director of the Czech Philharmonic Orchestra, a post he held for eighteen years. After immigrating to Canada in 1968, Ančerl was appointed music director of the Toronto Symphony Orchestra. *See also* Theresienstadt.

antisemitism Prejudice, discrimination, persecution and/or hatred against Jewish people, institutions, culture and symbols.

Appell (German) Roll call.

Auschwitz (German; in Polish, Oświęcim) A town in southern Poland approximately forty kilometres from Krakow, it is also the name of the largest complex of Nazi concentration camps that were built nearby. The Auschwitz complex contained three main camps: Auschwitz I, a slave labour camp built in May 1940; Auschwitz II-Birkenau, a death camp built in early 1942; and Auschwitz-Monowitz, a slave labour camp built in October 1942. In 1941, Auschwitz I was a testing site for usage of the lethal gas Zyklon B as a method of mass killing, which then went into wide usage. Between 1942 and 1944, transports arrived at Auschwitz-Birkenau from almost every country in Europe – hundreds of thousands from both Poland and Hungary, and thousands from France, the Netherlands, Greece, Slovakia, Bohemia and Moravia, Yugoslavia, Belgium, Italy and Norway. As well, more than thirty thousand people were deported there from other concentration camps. It is estimated that 1.1 million people were murdered in Auschwitz; approximately 950,000 were Jewish; 74,000 Polish; 21,000 Roma; 15,000 Soviet prisoners of war; and 10,000–15,000 other nationalities. The Auschwitz complex was liberated by the Soviet army in January 1945. *See also* Czech Family Camp.

Beneš, Edvard (1884–1948) The second and fourth president of Czechoslovakia (1935–38 and 1945–48). After Germany took control of part of Czechoslovakia in 1938, Beneš went into exile in Britain, where he formed the Czechoslovak government-in-exile. After the war, Beneš was reinstated as president until the Communist coup in February 1948; he resigned in June of that year and was succeeded by Communist leader Klement Gottwald. *See also* Gottwald, Klement.

Brundibár An opera composed in 1938 by Hans Krása and Adolf Hoffmeister that was performed by children in the Theresienstadt camp in September 1943. With its triumphant theme of good over evil, *Brundibár* was an important act of spiritual resistance; however, the opera was also performed during the ghetto's staged Red Cross visit, to show visitors that Jews were well treated. Throughout 1944, there were fifty-five performances in the camp. Over the past two decades, *Brundibár* has been showcased internationally multiple times. *See also* Theresienstadt.

Czech Family Camp (Auschwitz) A section of the Birkenau "quarantine" camp, where recent arrivals were housed temporarily, that was reserved for the more than 10,000 Czech-Jewish prisoners who were deported from the Theresienstadt camp between September and December 1943. For approximately six months, in an effort to counteract rumours that the Nazis were massacring Jews, the Czech Jews were accorded privileges such as receiving parcels and writing letters, but they were eventually subjected to the same fate as other prisoners at Birkenau. Thousands were murdered in the gas chambers on March 8 and 9, 1944; in July, after a selection that found only a few thousand of the prisoners fit for forced labour, the rest of the family camp, more than seven thousand Czech Jews, were murdered in the gas chambers. *See also* Theresienstadt.

Dachau The Nazis' first concentration camp, which was established primarily to house political prisoners in March 1933. The Dachau camp was located about sixteen kilometres northwest of Munich in southern Germany. The number of Jews interned there rose considerably after Kristallnacht pogroms on the night of November 9–10, 1938. By the spring of 1945, Dachau and its subcamps held more than 67,665 registered prisoners – 43,350 categorized as political prisoners and 22,100 as Jews. As the American Allied forces neared the camp in April 1945, the Nazis forced 7,000 prisoners, primarily Jews, on a gruelling death march to Tegernsee, a camp in southern Germany.

Dollfuss, Engelbert (1892–1934) Chancellor of Austria from 1932–1934. While in power, Dollfuss established an autocratic regime, Austrofascism, governed by the single-party, nationalistic Fatherland's Front and modelled on Mussolini's fascist party in Italy. Dollfuss advocated for Austrian independence; his anti-Nazi Party stance led to his assassination by Austrian Nazis on July 25, 1934.

Druze A monotheistic religious community in the Middle East.

Gestapo (German; abbreviation of Geheime Staatspolizei, the Secret State Police of Nazi Germany) The Gestapo were the brutal force that dealt with the perceived enemies of the Nazi regime and were responsible for rounding up European Jews for deportation to the death camps. They operated with very few legal constraints and were also responsible for issuing exit visas to the residents of German-occupied areas. A number of Gestapo members also joined the Einsatzgruppen, the mobile killing squads responsible for the roundup and murder of Jews in eastern Poland and the USSR through mass shooting operations.

Gottwald, Klement (1896–1953) The Czech communist politician who led the February 1948 non-violent seizure of power by the Communist Party in Czechoslovakia, which effectively ended democratic governance in Czechoslovakia until 1990. As president (1948–1953), Gottwald nationalized industries, collectivized farms, and purged the government of both non-communists and communists who were suspected of treason, which led to either their imprisonment or execution.

Haas, Pavel (1899–1944) A Czech-Jewish composer interned in the Theresienstadt camp, where he wrote eight compositions, from 1941 to 1944. Haas was deported to Auschwitz in 1944, and was sent to the gas chamber on arrival.

Hácha, Emil (1872–1945) President of Czechoslovakia from 1938–1939; under German occupation, Hácha effectively lost power. Hácha remained in office as a figurehead and was arrested as a collaborator after the war. He died in prison in June 1945.

kapo (German) A concentration camp prisoner appointed by the SS to oversee other prisoners as slave labourers.

König, Hans Wilhelm (1912–unknown) One of the SS doctors in Auschwitz during World War II, König was responsible for selections in the women's camp hospital; he also worked alongside the notorious Josef Mengele. *See also* Mengele, Josef.

Marx, Karl (1818–1883) The German philosopher, historian, sociologist and theorist who inspired the revolutionary communist ideology known as Marxism. His view of history, called "historical materialism," argued that capitalist modes of production that exploited workers would ultimately lead to a class struggle and a breakdown of the economy, laying the ground for communism.

According to Marx's vision, a communist society would be class-less and stateless, based on a common ownership of the means of production, free access to the material goods that people need for well-being, and an end to wage labour and private property. Two of his most famous books are *The Communist Manifesto* (1848) and *Capital* (1867–1894).

Masada The ancient fortification in the Judaean Desert in southern Israel that is a UNESCO World Heritage site. Masada was a significant symbol of Jewish rebellion at the end of the First Jewish-Roman War (66–73 CE), when 967 Jews held out against a Roman siege for three years at the top of the fortress. As it became evident that the Romans would prevail, most of the fighters, rather than be taken hostage by the Romans and sold as slaves, agreed to a suicide pact.

Masaryk, Jan (1886–1948) A liberal-democratic politician who was the son of Tomáš G. Masaryk, the founder and first president of Czechoslovakia. He served as foreign minister to the Czech government-in-exile during World War II, a position he retained in the provisional, multi-party National Front government established in Czechoslovakia after its liberation from the Germans in 1945. In 1948, following the consolidation of a Communist, Soviet-led government, Jan Masaryk was found dead in his pyjamas in the courtyard of his apartment building. There was ongoing debate and investigations into whether he committed suicide, as was proclaimed by the Communist government, or whether he was thrown to his death by Communist thugs. A final investigation, concluded in December 2003, proved that Masaryk was murdered through the testimony of an expert witness who studied the position of the body when it was found. This new evidence, however, did not lead to any prosecutions.

Masaryk, Tomáš Garrigue (1850–1937) The founder of Czechoslovakia and first president of the country, from 1918 to 1935. Masaryk recognized minority rights and was known for his strong public opposition to antisemitism; he came to symbolize democracy to Czech citizens and has been widely honoured posthumously.

Mauthausen A notoriously brutal Nazi concentration camp located about twenty kilometres east of the Austrian city of Linz. First established in 1936 shortly after the annexation of Austria to imprison "asocial" political opponents of the Third Reich, the camp grew to encompass fifty nearby subcamps and became the largest forced labour complex in the German-occupied territories. By the end of the war, close to 200,000 prisoners had passed through the Mauthausen forced labour camp system and almost 120,000 of them died there – including 38,120 Jews – from starvation, disease and hard labour. Mauthausen was classified as a Category 3 camp, which indicated the harshest conditions, and inmates were often worked to death in the brutal Weiner-Graben stone quarry. The US army liberated the camp on May 5, 1945.

Mengele, Josef (1911–1979) The most notorious of about thirty SS garrison physicians in Auschwitz. Mengele was stationed at the camp from May 1943 to January 1945; from May 1943 to August 1944, he was the medical officer of the Birkenau "Gypsy Camp"; from August 1944 until Auschwitz was evacuated in January 1945, he became Chief Medical Officer of the main infirmary camp in Birkenau. One of the camp doctors responsible for deciding which prisoners were fit for slave labour and which were to be immediately sent to the gas chambers, Mengele was also known for conducting sadistic experiments on Jewish and Roma prisoners, especially twins.

Miklas, Wilhelm (1872–1956) The president of Austria from 1928 to 1938, at which point the country was incorporated into Nazi Germany.

Rabbi Loew (1520–1609) Known as Judah Loew ben Bezalel, and also as the Maharal (a Hebrew acronym that translates to our teacher, Rabbi Loew) of Prague, Loew was a prominent Talmudic scholar, mystic and philosopher. He led congregations in the cities of both Mikulov and Prague.

Rabin, Yitzhak (1922–1995) An Israeli politician and member of parliament who was prime minister of Israel from 1974–1977 and 1992–1995. In 1994, Rabin was awarded the Nobel Peace Prize along with Shimon Peres and Yasser Arafat for their work on the Oslo Accords, a set of principles that outlined a peace process in the Middle East. Rabin was assassinated on November 5, 1995.

Rahm, Karl (1907–1947) The Commandant of the Theresienstadt camp from February 1944 until May 1945. Rahm supervised the propaganda film shot in the camp and oversaw deportations from Theresienstadt as well as the "beautification" of the camp to prepare for the Red Cross visit in June 1944. After liberation, Rahm was apprehended in Austria and put on trial in Czechoslovakia in 1947, where he was found guilty of war crimes and sentenced to death. *See also* Theresienstadt.

Ravensbrück The largest Nazi concentration camp created almost exclusively for women that was established in May 1939 and located about ninety kilometres north of Berlin. Throughout the war, subcamps were built in the area around Ravensbrück to serve as forced labour camps. From 1942 on, the complex served as one of the main training facilities for female SS guards. Medical experiments were carried out on the women at Ravensbrück and in early 1945 the SS built a gas chamber, where between 5,000 and 6,000 prisoners were murdered. More than 100,000 women prisoners from all over Nazi-occupied Europe had passed through Ravensbrück before the Soviets liberated the camp on April 29–30, 1945. Approximately 50,000 women died in the camp.

Righteous Among the Nations A title bestowed by Yad Vashem, the Holocaust Martyrs' and Heroes' Remembrance Authority in Jerusalem, to honour non-Jews who risked their lives to help save Jews during the Holocaust. A commission was established in 1963 to award the title. If a person fits certain criteria and the story is carefully corroborated, the honouree is awarded with a medal and certificate and commemorated on the Wall of Honour at the

Garden of the Righteous in Jerusalem.

Rosh Hashanah (Hebrew) New Year. The autumn holiday that marks the beginning of the Jewish year and ushers in the High Holy Days. It is observed by a synagogue service that ends with blowing the *shofar* (ram's horn), which marks the beginning of the holiday. The service is usually followed by a family dinner where sweet foods, such as apples and honey, are eaten to symbolize and celebrate a sweet new year.

Slánský, Rudolf (1901–1952) General Secretary of the Czech Communist Party from 1946 to 1951. Slánský, a Jew, had been active in the Czech Communist organization before the war, was involved in organizing the Slovak National Uprising of 1944 and, in 1946, took over the leadership of the Party. In 1951, he was suddenly ejected from the Party, accused of organizing a conspiracy to overthrow the government along with thirteen other Party members, ten of whom were also Jewish. Eleven of the accused were executed and three were given life sentences. All fourteen were officially exonerated in 1968.

Slovak National Uprising (August 29–October 28, 1944) The antifascist armed resistance mounted against the pro-Nazi Slovak government by partisans in central Slovakia. The uprising, comprised of approximately 80,000 partisans from more than thirty countries, was poorly planned and was crushed by German forces in two months, although battles continued in the area until the end of the war. An estimated 85,000 casualties resulted from the uprising, and Nazi troops destroyed ninety-three Slovak villages in retaliation for their suspected cooperation with partisan forces. In 1945, a square in the city of Banská Bystrica was dedicated to the uprising and in 1969, a memorial and museum opened to commemorate the uprising.

Sosúa A town in the Dominican Republic, the only country that was willing to accept a significant number of Jewish refugees during World War II. In 1940, the Dominican Republic government stated it would allow between 50,000 and 100,000 Jews to immigrate as agricultural workers; ultimately, only about six hundred Jews managed to settle in Sosúa.

Spielberg, Steven (1946–) An American film director who founded the Survivors of the Shoah Visual History Foundation in 1994, as a result of his experience making the film *Schindler's List*. The foundation records and preserves the testimonies of Holocaust survivors in a video archive and promotes Holocaust education. In 2006, after recording almost 50,000 international testimonies, the foundation partnered with the University of Southern California and became the USC Shoah Foundation Institute for Visual History and Education.

SS (abbreviation of Schutzstaffel; Defence Corps) The SS was established in 1925 as Adolf Hitler's elite corps of personal bodyguards. Under the direction of Heinrich Himmler, its membership grew from 280 in 1929 to 50,000 when the Nazis came to power in 1933, and to nearly a quarter of a million on the eve of World War II. The SS was comprised of the Allgemeine-SS (General SS) and the Waffen-SS (Armed, or Combat SS). The General SS dealt with policing and the enforcement of Nazi racial policies in Germany and the Nazi-occupied countries. An important unit within the SS was the Reichssicherheitshauptamt (RSHA, the Central Office of Reich Security), whose responsibility included the Gestapo (Geheime Staatspolizei). The SS ran the concentration and death camps, with all their associated economic enterprises, and also fielded its own Waffen-SS military divisions, including some recruited from the occupied countries. *See also* Gestapo.

Theresienstadt (German; in Czech, Terezín) A walled town in the Czech Republic sixty kilometres north of Prague that served as both a ghetto and a concentration camp. More than 73,000 Jews from the German Protectorate of Bohemia and Moravia and from the Greater German Reich (including Austria and parts of Poland) were deported to Theresienstadt between 1941 and 1945, 60,000 of whom were deported to Auschwitz or other death camps. Theresienstadt was showcased as a "model" ghetto for propaganda purposes to demonstrate to delegates from the International Red Cross and others the "humane" treatment of Jews and to counter information reaching the Allies about Nazi atrocities and mass murder. Theresienstadt was liberated on May 8, 1945 by the Soviet Red Army.

Tiso, Father Jozef (1887–1947) The pro-Nazi Slovak cleric who became head of the fascist Slovak state from 1939 to 1945.

Treaty of Versailles One of the five treaties produced at the 1919 Paris Peace Conference organized by the victors of World War I. The Treaty of Versailles imposed a harsh and punitive peace on Germany, including high reparations, restrictions on German military rearmament and activities, and the redrawing of Germany's borders, which resulted in the loss of territory.

Trudeau, Pierre (1919–2000) Prime minister of Canada from 1968–1979 and 1980–1984, Trudeau is often remembered for establishing official policies on federal bilingualism and multiculturalism, and entrenching the Canadian Charter of Rights in 1982.

Union of Czechoslovak Youth An organization established by the Communist Party for youth between ages fifteen and twenty-five, whose purpose was to promote membership in the Communist Party.

Vietnam War The conflict between North Vietnam and US-supported South Vietnam that took place between November 1955 and April 1975.

Yad Vashem The Holocaust Martyrs' and Heroes' Remembrance Authority established in 1953 to commemorate, educate the public about, research and document the Holocaust.

Yiddish A language derived from Middle High German with elements of Hebrew, Aramaic, Romance and Slavic languages, and written in Hebrew characters. Spoken by Jews in east-central Europe for roughly a thousand years from the tenth century to the mid-twentieth century, it was still the most common language among European Jews until the outbreak of World War II. There are similarities between Yiddish and contemporary German.

Photographs

1 & 2 Gerta Solan's paternal grandparents, Zigmund and Amalia Gelbkopf.
3 Klara and Friedrich (Fritz) Roubitschek, Gerta's maternal grandparents.

1 Gerta and Grandpa Fritz in Prague, circa 1933.
2 Grete and Theodor, Gerta's parents, in Prague. Date unknown.
3 Gerta, approximately 3 years old, with her parents.

1 & 2 Gerta's uncle Franz Roubitschek and Aunt Anny.

3 & 4 Gerta's aunt Irma and uncle Josef Kantor.

1   Gerta's uncle Paul Roubitschek, her mother's youngest brother.
2   Gerta (front, seated) with her extended family. In the back row (left to right) are her uncle Paul, grandfather Fritz and grandmother Klara; front row (left to right) are Paul's girlfriend, Zdenka; Gerta's mother, Grete; and Gerta's cousin Ella.
3   On vacation at the Prachovské Rocks, Czechoslovakia. Left to right: Grete; Gerta; cousin Ella; Ella's friend; and Zdenka.
4   Gerta and her cousin Ella.

Gerta Solan, circa 1941.

Paul and Gerta's wedding photo. Banská Bystrica, April 11, 1949.

1 & 2 Paul's parents, Jolana (Joly) and Maximilian (Miška) Solan.
3 Gerta's brother-in-law, Peter Solan.
4 Peter and Micka's wedding.

1   Paul and Gerta at the airport, waiting to immigrate to Toronto. Vienna, 1968.
2   At the Vienna airport with her son, Michal (Mišhko).
3   Gerta and Paul outside Thorncliffe Park Drive, their second home in Toronto, in
    the early 1970s.
4   Gerta and Mišhko in their new apartment, circa 1970.

Gerta and Paul, 1980.

1 & 2 Gerta's grandchildren Yarko (left) and Daniel (right).

1

2

3

1   Luci and Vilko Schönfeld, Gerta and Paul's close friends.
2   Gerta's friends Laco and the "older" Věra, who was with Gerta in Rechlin, Germany.
3   Gerta's friends from the Red Cross. Left to right: Theresa, John, Winn and Grace; with Gerta's friend Hana (right), whom she met in Theresienstadt.

THE
YELLOW
ROSE
PROJECT

Toronto's 4th Annual Senior Prom
June 18, 2013

A recent photo of Gerta Solan at the prom for Holocaust survivors put on by the
Yellow Rose Project. Toronto, 2013.

Index

Acs, Irena, 71, 73, 74, 78, 80
Acs, Katka, 71
Acs, Mirka, 77
Acs, Pišta (Steve), 71, 72, 73, 74, 77, 78, 80
Agi (colleague), 126
AGO (Art Gallery of Ontario), 127
Aida confectionery, Vienna, 9
Akko (Israel), 100
Alcron hotel (Prague), 54, 63, 64
Amir, Yigal, 137
Anca (Jolana Solan's sister), 50
Ančerl, Karel, 20, 22
Anička (friend), 102
Anna (Red Cross), 86–87
antisemitism: in 1940s
    Czechoslovakia, 14–16; in 1950s
    Czechoslovakia, 53–54; among
    Ravensbrück inmates, 31
Appell (roll call), 26, 30
Aranka, (Paul's aunt), 117
Auergesellschaft company, 7
Auschwitz (Birkenau): children's
    barracks in, 26–27; crematoria

in, 25, 28; Czech "family camp"
in, xxiii, 19; family deaths in,
20, 30; liquidation of, 30; living
conditions in, 25–27; music in,
29; transportation of Czech Jews
to, xxii–xxiii, 18–19, 23; work
detail in, 27, 28
Austria: assassination of Dollfuss,
10; civil war in, 10; German occupation of, 9
Avenue of the Righteous Among
the Nations (Yad Vashem), 135
Baarová, Lída, 5
Banská Bystrica, 49
Barrandov film studio, 5
bat mitzvah, 111–112
Bauhof (lumberyard), 17
Bedřich (Stella's husband), 100
Bela (Jolana Solan's brother), 49–50
Beneš, Edvard, 45
Berlin (Germany), 37–38
Birkenau. See Auschwitz
    (Birkenau).
block elders, 26, 29

"The Blue Guitar" (Tippett), 127
Bohušovice, 20
Brabec, Jaroslav (chauffeur), 60
Brno (Czechoslovakia), 3, 10, 26
Brundibár (children's opera), xxi,
　21, 22
Bush, George W., 111, 112
Caesarea (Israel), 100
Cake Master (Toronto), 78–79
camps. See also Auschwitz;
　Theresienstadt; Birkenau, 19;
　Dachau, 91–92; Mauthausen, 39;
　Oranienburg, 31; Ravensbrück,
　31
Canadian Red Cross, 84–91, 106,
　125–126
Carpatho-Ukraine area, 13
cattle wagons, 23, 30–31
census taking (Theresienstadt), 20
Černy, Ella, 41
Černy, Rolland, 41, 99, 123
Černy, Ron, 41, 123
Chagall, Marc, 134
Children's Memorial Hall (Yad
　Vashem), 135
Chinatown (Toronto), 72
Christine (colleague), 127
Chrudimská Street (Prague), 4
Cole, Nat King, 118
Cole, Natalie, 118
communism: Czechoslovakia
　under, xxvi–xxviii, 45–46, 53–57,
　66; Gerta's views on, 55–57
Communist Party, 10, 45–46, 53–57,
　66
Czech Republic, 131

Czechoslovak National Association
　(Toronto), 105
Czechoslovak National Socialist
　Party, 45
Czechoslovakia. See also Prague;
　antisemitism in, xv, 14–16, 53–
　54; anti-Jewish laws in, xvi–xvii;
　Communist Party 1946 win, 45;
　under communist rule, xxvi–
　xxviii, 45–46, 53–57, 66; Czech
　Republic realities, 131; death of
　Masaryk in, 11–12; Jewish emi-
　gration from, xxv; Nazi occupa-
　tion of, xvi, 13–14; pre-war, xiii–
　xv; Slovak National Uprising,
　44; Slovakia's separation from,
　xvi, 13; Soviet invasion of, 63–65;
　Soviet liberation of, 34–35; trea-
　son show trial in, 53–54
Bruno (cousin; Karl's son), 92
Dachau, 91–92
Danish Ministry of Health, 21–22
Danish Red Cross, 21–22
death camps. See Auschwitz.
Dennis (colleague), 126
deportation: from Auschwitz, 30–31;
　from Prague, 16; from Rechlin,
　33; from Theresienstadt camp, 23
Diamond, Jack, 134
Dizengoff Street (Tel Aviv), 100
Dlouhá 19 (Prague), 14
Dobrý voják Švejk (Hašek), 56
Dollfuss, Englebert (Austrian chan-
　cellor), 10
Donna (colleague), 126, 127
Dubček, Alexander (Prague

Spring), xxviii
Eda (Gabi's husband), 81
education: under communism, 55, 57; in Jewish quarter, 15; at *Mädchenheim*, 18
Emmy (cousin; Karl's wife), 91–92, 117
Ephesus, 108
Eppstein, Dr. (Council of Elders), 21–22
Erben, Peter, 30, 47–48
Eva (from Trenčín), 32
Fatherland's Front party, 10
Fechtner, Karel, 11
Fernando (Cuban friend), 88
forced labour, 17, 18, 27, 28, 31
Frič, Martin, 5
Friedlander, Mrs., 16
Fröhlich, Gustav, 5
The Führer Gives the Jews a City, 22
Gabi (from Auschwitz), 81
Galambos, Mató, 136
Gelbkopf, Amalia (grandmother), 10–11, 19
Gelbkopf, Gerta. *See* Solan, Gerta.
Gelbkopf, Grete (mother) (née Roubitschek): courage, xvii, 13–14, 15, 23; early memories of, 3–6; fate, 39; family history, xiv; jobs at Theresienstadt, 17–18; siblings, 6; stoicism, 20
Gelbkopf, Sigmund (grandfather), 10–11, 19
Gelbkopf, Theodor (Teddy) (father): early memories of, 3–6, 13–14; family history, xiv; job at

camp, 17–18; disappearance of, 23; death of, 30
George (friend), 102
George Brown College, 83–84
Georgina, 126
German civilians, 30, 33, 34, 37, 130
German Foreign Office, 21–22
German Protectorate of Bohemia and Moravia, 13, 22
German Red Cross, 21–22
Germany: annexation of Austria by, 10; Berlin, 37–38; occupation of Czechoslovakia, xv–xvi, 13–14; reparations from, 70–71; in retreat, 30–33
Gerron, Kurt, xxi, 22
Gershwin, George, 79, 117
Gerti (housemaid for Franz Roubitschek), 70
Gestapo, 15
Ginny (boss), 126, 127
Glenn Gould studio, 127–128
Gold, Karol, 72–73
The Good Soldier Švejk (Hašek), 56
Gottwald, Klement, 45–46, 53
Grace (Red Cross volunteer), 90
Greece, 107–108
Green, Anna (Nushi), 80–81, 98, 114, 126, 127
Green, Jana, 81
Green, Yurko, 81
Green, Zoli, 80–81, 98, 126
Gulf War, 111–112
Haas, Pavel, 20
Hácha, Emil, 13
Hagibor sports club, xvii, 15

Hamburg barracks, 17–18, 23
Hana (from Theresienstadt),
    102–103
Harbourfront Centre (Toronto), 21
Havel, Václav, 5, 110
Havel, Maria, 5
Heimwehr (Austrian Home
    Defence Force), 10
Herzog, Chaim, 109
Hirsch, Fredy, 16, 18–19
Hitler, Adolf, xv, 8, 10, 13
Hlaváčová (school), 43
Hoffmeister, Adolf, 21
Holland Mill coffee house (Prague),
    5
Horna, Janko, 74
Horna, Lolla, 74, 78
Horna, Yurko, 74
Hotel Alcron, 54
Hungary, xv, xvi, xxv
hunger: courage in the face of, 17,
    33; desperation in face of, 19,
    28–29, 32; effects on Gerta of, 35,
    39; Gerta's reaction to, 17, 18, 19,
    22, 29, 30, 32, 33
Hussein, Saddam, 111
Hvass, Franz, 21
Hybernská Street (Prague), 5
IBM, 59–60, 67–68, 69
Ilana Goor, 136
International Red Cross, 21–22
Israel: Gulf War threat, 111–112;
    Michal Solan in, 96–97, 98,
    101, 106, 123–124; recruiting
    of European refugees by, 70;
    Solans' visits to, 98–101, 109–110,

122–124, 131–136; World Rally of
    Czechoslovak Jews, 109–111
Jaffa, 100, 136
Janáček, Mr. (camp guard), 19
Janko (Růženka's son), 50
Jano (Růženka's husband), 50
Jerusalem, 132, 133–134
Jewish cemetery (Prague), 14–15
Jewish Council of Elders, xix, 17, 21
Jewish ghetto. See Theresienstadt
    camp.
Ježek, Jaroslav, 18
Jiranek (store) (Prague), 7
John (Red Cross volunteer), 90–91,
    126–127
Johnson, Miss, 85
Jonas, George, 78
Jos (Red Cross), 86, 87
Juel-Henningsen, Dr. E., 21
Kafka, Franz, 14
Kaja (Hana Schönfeld's husband),
    124, 135
Kantor, Irma (aunt), 9
Kantor, Josef (uncle), 9
Kantor, Lizzy (cousin), 9–10
Kantor, Quido (cousin), 10
kapo (foreman), 29
Karl (father's cousin), 11, 91–92, 117
Karvaš, Peter, 66
Kathy (from Theresienstadt),
    102–103
kibbutzim (community farms), 96,
    100
Kiely, Helen, 88–89
Knesset, 134
Kollek, Teddy, 110

König, Dr. Hans Wilhelm, 25
Krása, Hans, 21
Kraus, Dr., 81
Kremnička, 51
Křižovnická 3 (Prague), 4
Küerti, Prof., 70
Kusadasi, 108
Laci (friend), 114
Lajos (Ella's partner), 6
Lány (Prague), 11
Leaside High School, 96
Loew, Rabbi, 15
"Lost Composers," 21
Lucille (friend from Trinidad), 88
Lucky, Stefan, 70, 110
Maccabi Hatzair exercise hall, xvii, 15
Mädchenheim (girls' home), 18
"The Man I Love" (Gershwin), 117
Manpower (Toronto), 73, 74, 83
Mary (secretary), 126
Masada, 101
Masaryk, Jan, 45–46
Masaryk, Tomáš Garrigue, 11–12, 19
Matys, Mr. (baker in Prague), 16
Mauthausen, 39
Max (Open Window Bakery), 75–76
Maxwell, Robert, 109
McClory, Ron, 88
memoirs, 1–2, 119, 132
Mengele, Josef, 25
Miklas, Wilhelm (president of Austria), 10
Mila (Stefan Lucky's friend), 70
Millie (friend from Red Cross), 88, 126
Montefiore, Moses Haim, 134
Mount Sinai Hospital, 113
music: in Auschwitz, 29; *Brundibár* (children's opera), xxi, 21, 22; in family home, 3; Glenn Gould studio, 127–128; at Harbourfront Centre, 21; during restrictions in Prague, 16; Spring International Music Festival, 58; Summer Jazz Festival, 128; Telefunken, 79; at Theresienstadt camp, 18, 20–21, 22
Mussolini, Benito, 10
Národní Avenue (Prague), 4, 43
Nazis, 13–14, 16, 44, 103
Neustrelitz (Germany), 34
Nicholas (cousin; Karl's son), 92
Night and Day (Gershwin), 79
Novak, Lily, 80
Open Window Bakery (Toronto), 75–76, 101, 117
Operation Desert Storm, 111, 112
Oranienburg camp, 31
Patmos, 108
Pegasus (ship), 108–109
Platnéřská Street (Prague), 14
Pleta (store) (Prague), 4
Podmokly (Czechoslovakia), 38
Prague. *See also* Czechoslovakia; in 1995, 129, 130–131; deportation of Jews from, xvii, 16; old Prague, 54; pre-war; xiii; restrictions on Jews in, 14–16, 56; show trial set in, xxvii, 53–54; theatres, 56; visits to, 121–122, 129–131

Prater amusement park (Vienna), 9
Price, Mr., 85, 87
Puerto Plata, 104
Rabin, Yitzak, 137
Rahm, Karl, 22, 23
Rámová 1 (Prague), 13
Raumwirtschaft office, 17
Ravensbrück camp, xxiv, 31
Rechlin (Retzow) (Germany), xxiv, 31–33
Red Cross: Canadian national office, 85–88, 106; Danish, 21–22; reorganization of Canadian, 125–126; Toronto branch of, 88–89, 106; Toronto mandate, 89–90; visit to Theresienstadt of, 21–22; volunteering with, 91
red triangle, 31
Redlich, Egon, xxii
Rigor, Georgina, 78–79
Rigor, Paul, 78–79
Rossel, Maurice, 21, 22
Rotem (Michal Solan's partner), 133
Roubitschek, Anny (aunt), xxv, 8–9, 49
Roubitschek, Edith (cousin), 6, 39, 40–41
Roubitschek, Ella (cousin), 6, 34. *See also* Černy, Ella.
Roubitschek, Erwin (uncle), 6
Roubitschek, Franz (Franzl) (uncle), xxv, 6, 8–9, 49, 68, 70
Roubitschek, Friedrich (Fritz) (grandfather), xix, 6–8, 19, 20
Roubitschek, Grete (mother). *See* Gelbkopf, Grete.

Roubitschek, Hans (uncle), 6
Roubitschek, Klara (grandmother), 6–8, 19, 20
Roubitschek, Paul (uncle), 6, 7–8
Rush, Mr., 87
Russian P O W s (prisoners of war), 32
Růženka (Jolana Solan's maid), 50
Sacher Kaffeehaus (Vienna), 9
Santorini, 107–108
Schanzer, George, 70
Schanzer, Juca, 117
Schanzer, Judith, 70
Schindler's List, 1
Schönberg, Arnold, 91
Schönfeld, Eva, 124, 136
Schönfeld, Hana, 124, 130, 136
Schönfeld, Luci, 47, 66, 100, 103, 109–111, 122–123, 135–136,
Schönfeld, Vilko, 47, 58, 66, 100, 110, 115, 123
Schubert, Franz, 11, 117
Schutzbund, 10
Seidner, Paul. *See* Solan, Paul.
Sermer family, 71
Shani (Alex) (colleague), 126
Simpson, Mrs., 85, 86, 87
Slánský, Rudolf, xxvii, 53
Slovak National Uprising (August 1944), 44
Slovakia, xv, xxiv–xxv
Social Democratic Party, Austria, 10
Solan, Daniel (Danielko) (grandson), 104, 124, 132–133, 137–138
Solan, Dominika, 105, 106
Solan, Gerta (née Gelbkopf): child-

hood in Prague, 3–12; during restrictions in Prague, 15–16; at Theresienstadt camp, xix–xx; 16–23; at Auschwitz, xxiii, 25–30; on death march, xxiv, 30, 33–34; liberation from Auschwitz, 34–35; at Ravensbrück camp, 31; Rechlin, 31–32; return to Prague, 37–42; courtship and marriage, 44–45, 46–52; pregnancy, 52; birth of Michal, 58–59; employment in Prague, 46, 54–55, 59–60; education/training, 11, 43, 51, 83–84; post-war antisemitism, effects on, 55; communism, views on, 55–57; escape to Vienna, 65–67, 69–70; immigration to Toronto, xxviii, 71–72; early days in Toronto, 72–77; getting established in Toronto, 93, 98; employment in Toronto, 75–76, 78–79, 84–88; illness and death of Paul, 108–109, 113–119; retiring, 125–127

Solan, Hana (daughter-in-law), 96–97, 101–102, 104, 106, 124

Solan, Iveta (Ivo's first wife), 104–106

Solan, Ivo (Peter's son), 104–106, 114

Solan, Jolana (Joly) (mother-in-law), 48, 49–50, 60–61, 94

Solan, Lenka (Ivo's second wife), 106, 116

Solan, Maria (Micka) (Peter's wife), 51, 66–67, 104, 122

Solan, Maximilian (Miška) (father-in-law), 48, 50–51, 60

Solan, Michal (Miško) (son): early years in Prague, 58–59, 60, 61, 65, 67–68; athletics, 60, 61, 92–93; education, post-secondary, 97, 101; birth of children, 104; discrimination faced by, 95; in Israel, 96–97, 98, 101, 106, 123–124; marriage, 97; reaction to memoirs, 1–2, 67–68; schools, 59, 60–61, 76–77, 95–96; separation, 124; in Toronto, 113, 116–117, 124

Solan, Paul: war experience, 44; professional training, 44, 51; antisemitism, effects on, 54; escapes to Vienna, 65–67, 69–70; immigration to Toronto, 71–72; work in Toronto, 75–76, 78; trips abroad, 98–101, 103–104, 105–106, 107–108, 109–110; cancer treatment, 108–109, 113–116; death of, 116

Solan, Peter (Paul's brother), 44, 66–67, 122

Solan, Yair (Yarko) (grandson), 104, 124, 132–133, 137–138

Sosúa (Dominican Republic), 103–104

Soviet soldiers, 30, 34, 37, 64–65, 68

Soviet Union: invasion of Czechoslovakia by, xxviii, 63–65; involvement in Czech politics by, 45–46, 53–54, 63; liberation of Czechoslovakia by, 30, 34–35

Spielberg, Steven, 1

Spring International Music Festival,
57, 58
SS (Schutzstaffel), 20, 22, 27, 31, 33
Stanley (Jos's husband), 86
Star of David, xvii, 15, 31
Stella (Paul Solan's cousin), 100
Stern, Eva (friend), 27, 30, 31, 32–33
Steve (Paul's cousin), 117
Strafblock (prison barracks), 31
Strašnice district (Prague), 15
Strešovice Street (Prague), 15
Šumava (Czech Republic), 128,
129–130
Summer Jazz Festival (Toronto), 128
Susi (friend), 124
Szuësz, Cornel, 75
Szuësz-Gold, Věra (small Věra), 32,
33, 34, 43, 71–73, 111
Technomat, 55
Tel Aviv, 100–101, 112
Terezín. *See* Theresienstadt camp.
Theresa (Red Cross), 87
Theresienstadt camp: culture/
resistance in, xx–xxii; family
deaths in, 19; living conditions
in, xviii, 17–21; location, xvii, 16;
Nazi propaganda in, xx, 22, 135;
population, 1942, xviii, 17; Red
Cross visit to, xx–xxi, 21–22;
survival rate of children, 2; work
detail, 17, 18
Thorncliffe Park Drive, 80
Tiso, Jozef (Slovak premier), 13
Toronto Transit Commission
(TTC), 73, 128
Trade Fair Palace (Prague), 16
Trudeau, Pierre, 71

Turkey, 108
"Two Thousand Words," 66
"Unfinished Symphony" (Schubert),
11, 117
"Unforgettable" (Nat King Cole and
Natalie Cole), 118
Union of Czechoslovak Women, 46
Union of Czechoslovak Youth, 46
Veblová (store) (Prague), 5
Věra ("older," from Trenčin). *See*
Zeman, Věra.
Věra ("small"). *See* Szuësz-Gold,
Věra.
Vienna, xiii, xiv, 8, 9, 105
Vilma (from Vienna), 7
Vinohrady district (Prague), 4, 38,
58
Vinohradská Street (Prague), 43
Voskovec, Jiří, 18
Warren, Sarah, 85
Warsaw Pact, 63
Weber, George, 86
Wenceslas Square, 64, 65, 130
Werich, Jan, 18
Werner family, 81
World Rally of Czechoslovak Jews,
109–111
Yad Vadshem, 134–135
Zdenka (Uncle Paul's girlfriend),
7–8
Zeman, Hana, 47
Zeman, Jirka, 47
Zeman, Laco, 46–47, 66, 121–122,
129–130
Zeman, Věra, 32, 33, 34, 38, 43,
46–47, 121–122, 129–130, 138
Zoli (colleague), 126

The Azrieli Foundation was established in 1989 to realize and extend the philanthropic vision of David J. Azrieli, C.M., C.Q., M.Arch. The Foundation's mission is to support a wide spectrum of initiatives in education and research. The Azrieli Foundation is an active supporter of programs in the fields of Education, the education of architects, scientific and medical research, and the arts. The Azrieli Foundation's many initiatives include: the Holocaust Survivor Memoirs Program, which collects, preserves, publishes and distributes the written memoirs of survivors in Canada; the Azrieli Institute for Educational Empowerment, an innovative program successfully working to keep at-risk youth in school; the Azrieli Fellows Program, which promotes academic excellence and leadership on the graduate level at Israeli universities; the Azrieli Music Project, which celebrates and fosters the creation of high-quality new Jewish orchestral music; and the Azrieli Neurodevelopmental Research Program, which supports advanced research on neurodevelopmental disorders, particularly Fragile X and Autism Spectrum Disorders.